BEWARE WHAT LIES BEYOND

RED RIDING HOOD
FROM SCRIPT to SCREEN

INSIGHT ◉ EDITIONS

San Rafael, California

SHERRIFF

by director CATHERINE HARDWICKE
screenplay written by DAVID LESLIE JOHNSON

INSIGHT EDITIONS

10 Paul Dr.
San Rafael, CA 94903
www.insighteditions.com

Library of Congress Cataloging-in-Publication Data available.

ISBN: 978-1-60887-023-3

ROOTS of PEACE ⊕ REPLANTED PAPER

Insight Editions, in association with Roots of Peace, will plant
two trees for each tree used in the manufacturing of this book.
Roots of Peace is an internationally renowned humanitarian
organization dedicated to eradicating land mines worldwide and
converting war-torn lands into productive farms and wildlife
habitats. Together, we will plant two million fruit and nut trees
in Afghanistan and provide farmers there with the skills and
support necessary for sustainable land use.

Manufactured in China

10 9 8 7 6 5 4 3 2 1

CONTENTS

INTRODUCTION

Red Riding Hood is my dream job. I've been creating my own world since I was a little kid—little wooden "tiny towns" in a mountain of "carrot dirt" that my dad brought home from the farm and dumped in our backyard. My dolls used to take vacations on the moon in the pots and pans from the kitchen. And I drew every day: alien creatures (the Booma-Cooma, the Three-Balled-Jeanna), detailed villages built on stilts, orphanages full of exceptional kids—weird stuff. As an architect, I found most people to be conservative in their buildings—more concerned with the resale value than the originality. So I came to Hollywood, and I've finally had a chance to create a unique world on film. On this page is my earliest sketch

of the Daggörhorn Village, inspired by a little book of Russian architecture that I've saved since I was a teenager. I drew cottages raised on stilts, with spikes and animal totems on the roofs—a visual representation of the town's paranoia and fear of the wolf. Illustrator Kit Stolen colored the drawing, creating a magical atmosphere. When Warner Bros. "greenlit" the movie, a crazy talented group of artists— from the U.S., Canada, and Australia—worked to bring the world to life. Included in this book is a sampling of the storyboards, concept illustrations, costume designs, prop sketches, blueprints, set photos, and some my early paintings—all working to bring a new take to this classic fairy tale.

Catherine Hardwicke

FADE IN:

OPENING CREDITS play over a haunting melody as...

WE DRIFT HIGH ABOVE ALPINE GLACIERS...

...and SOAR OVER snow-capped MOUNTAINS...

...passing a rugged FORT tucked into an impossibly high summit,
then...

...a turquoise lake frozen solid, surrounding a heart-shaped
island...

...and we drop in elevation, below the snowline, to find a
thriving medieval METROPOLIS, unlike any we've ever seen, with
spiraling stone towers.

The city hugs a lakeshore brimming with majestic wooden sailboats
ferrying cargo...

...and we fly low, skimming the surface of the lake, and suddenly
plunge down over a waterfall, spilling torrents into the verdant
valley below...

..and we follow an EAGLE, just for a moment, as it SOARS over the
hick pine forest, following a winding river, then...

..settles on the highest branch of the TALLEST PINE.

he sky is strangely beautiful, like sunrise after a storm. It's
pringtime, and the trees are alight with dark green leaves. Larks
hirp in new nests.

his is a fairy tale world, a place where all our dreams and
ightmares are real. The light is bright, blown out. The light of
EMORY.

We flew in a helicopter over the stunning
mountains north of Vancouver. Adding
castles and cities into the crazy-beautiful
mist helped create the fairy tale world...

SHERRIFF

SHERRIFF

Now we drop down from the tallest pine, FINDING...

A SMALL GOTHIC VILLAGE nestled in the green valley. This isn't like
any medieval village we've ever seen. There's a large inn with a
lookout tower. A prosperous Blacksmith's Shop. A log Church and
a graveyard crowded with elongated headstones. The whole town is
surrounded by a high wall made of logs impaled in the ground, the

the village of **Daggörtorn**

The houses are not your typical peasant huts. They're
made of sturdy lumber and built on stilts. They have
HEAVY SHUTTERS on the windows and carved animal TOTEMS
to ward off demons, and some even have SPIKES sticking
out of their roofs. These homes look like miniature forts.

But even with the village's fortifications, beauty emerges.
Wildflowers grow through cracks in the stones.

CREDITS END.

Walking down a mean little street is a young girl, VALERIE (7), swinging a water pail. She's already a <u>bewitching beauty</u> with fierce green eyes, dressed in the BRITCHES of a TOMBOY and wearing a carved bone necklace.

The young girl passes a wooden sign: a <u>THREE QUARTERS MOON</u>. A strapping man, THE REEVE (40), replaces the sign with an <u>ANGRY FULL MOON</u>.

Beside the sign is a pagan WOLF TEMPLE: tall stones <u>set around a SACRIFICIAL ALTAR</u>.

SHERRIFF

Valerie watches as a FARMER chains a PIG up to the altar. His
DAUGHTER (5) cries.

                              THE REEVE
              Better the Wolf takes the pig than
              you, dear.

Valerie walks away quickly, out through the back gate,
and heads toward a STREAM.

YOUNG VALERIE

VALERIE

originally we wanted
Valerie to have dark hair...

14

set illustrations by Dean Sherriff

VALERIE

spring look

YOUNG PETER

fall look - 10 years later

PETER

costume illustrations by Kit Stølen

Suddenly—WHOOSH! A Boy JUMPS out in front of her, scaring the shit out of her. It's PETER (11), tan, muscular.

> YOUNG PETER
> Did you bring it?

Valerie looks around. Nobody's watching. She reaches into her pocket and pulls out a SHINY RED APPLE. Peter smiles and grabs her hand. They dash into the woods.

EXT. DARK FOREST - GREAT PINE - DAY - SPRING

In this MEMORY, there is an enormous PINE TREE that stands broader and more gnarled than the woods around it. WE HEAR the two children trying to control their giggles and *shh*ing each other.

We find Valerie and Peter nestled in the roots of the Great Pine. Lying on their stomachs next to each other, leaves in their hair. Whispering.

> YOUNG VALERIE
> Peter... do you have the knife?

> PETER
> Right here.

Peter whips out a SHARP LITTLE KNIFE. Their bodies right next to each other. But their attention is on a CRUDE ANIMAL TRAP. The kids watch a WHITE RABBIT hop up to the trap. They hold their breath as it takes the bait—a piece of the SHINY RED APPLE. SNAP.

The kids scramble up out of hiding. Giddy over their conquest, building on each other's enthusiasm...

> YOUNG VALERIE
> Look—snow white fur—

> YOUNG PETER
> I'll make us a pair of hunting
> boots—

16

Their breath comes fast, their eyes flash with a hunter's triumph. Little savages. Then they step closer to what they've caught and see that it is a WARM, LIVING THING.

Valerie and Peter look at each other. It is not a child's game anymore. The rabbit twitches, scared for its life. Peter reaches for it.

                    YOUNG PETER
          Its heart is beating so fast.

                    YOUNG VALERIE
          What do we do now...?

They both look at the knife in Peter's hand, then look at each other...

CAMERA PUSHES IN on VALERIE'S INTENSE GREEN EYES...

EXT. FOREST CLEARING - DAY - 10 YEARS LATER

TIGHT ON A DARK TREE TRUNK—a girl with those SAME INTENSE GREEN EYES steps out. The same bone necklace. Valerie is now 17 years old—a staggeringly beautiful young woman. She stands in the forest shadows, looking toward a clearing, spying through the branches...

Her POV: SEVEN WOODSMEN, including Valerie's FATHER (40), are working to bring down MASSIVE TREES. Valerie's eyes are fixed on one young man in particular:

PETER (now 21), darkly handsome, powerfully built. He doesn't see Valerie. She watches him work, enjoying the view. She smiles. Excited. Young and in love.

The Woodsmen break for lunch. Peter finally stops and BURIES HIS AXE IN A STUMP and goes to get water.

17

VALERIE

PETER

EXT. FIELD OF HAYSTACKS - DAY

A gentle breeze blows over a freshly harvested field of
haystacks, tangled up with blue cornflowers. WE HEAR a
SOFT HUMMING... and find CLAUDE (15). Red haired,
sensitive. Claude sits opposite a little Scarecrow made
out of hay.

The Scarecrow holds some TAROT CARDS in its "hand."
Claude plucks a card and makes it "disappear." Simple
sleight-of-hand. The Scarecrow stares blankly.

If he was born today, he'd probably be placed somewhere
on the <u>autism spectrum</u>. Here, we just get a sense that
he's... *different*.

20

WE HEAR the wind through the hay, and Claude's humming. WE
HEAR the rhythmic chopping of AXES, taking us back to—

EXT.   FOREST CLEARING - DAY

Break is over. Peter heads back to the stump where he
left his axe. <u>It's gone.</u>

Peter stops short. The other men are distracted. He walks
toward the forest, unnoticed...

EXT. FIELD OF HAYSTACKS - DAY

Claude flips a tarot card up in the air and it is CAUGHT
BY THE BREEZE. He follows it through the haystacks. HUMS.

EXT. DARK FOREST - GREAT PINE - DAY

Peter walks deeper and sees that giant Pine, the one from
the Memory. But now, Valerie stands under the Pine, holding
Peter's axe. Giving him a look that would launch a thousand
ships. Peter shoots one right back at her.

                    PETER
          Give me that.

                    VALERIE
          (seductive, playful)
          What will you give me for it?

But Peter doesn't smile. In fact, his face darkens.
Valerie isn't sure what to make of it. He steps toward
her, but she backs into the Pine. Peter steps up VERY
CLOSE BUT NOT TOUCHING. He searches for something on
her face but doesn't find it. He strokes her cheek.

PETER
They didn't tell you.

VALERIE
Tell me what?

EXT. FIELD OF HAYSTACKS - DAY

Claude, humming louder, moves faster through the
hay. The wind keeps the tarot card just out of
his reach. But now he GRABS it and makes an odd
little SOUND OF TRIUMPH. He smiles, but then...
he SEES dark stains in the trampled hay. He
follows the stains. Still humming.

EXT. DARK FOREST - GREAT PINE - DAY

Peter looks at Valerie. He's serious now.

PETER
Your mother brought breakfast to
the men this morning.

VALERIE

I know. I had to help make the
biscuits. Mine were the lumpy ones.

PETER

I heard her talking to your father.
They've arranged for you to marry
Henry Lazar.

VALERIE

So, Mother finally got what she
wanted. Some money.

PETER

And Henry gets what he's always
wanted. You.

VALERIE

What do we do now?

PETER

Do you want to marry him?

VALERIE

You know I don't.

PETER

Prove it.

VALERIE

How?

PETER

Run away with me.

Valerie reacts, surprised.

VALERIE

Where would we go?

PETER

Anywhere you want. The ocean, the
city, the mountains...

Valerie hesitates. Peter sees it.

PETER

You're afraid.

                    VALERIE
          No, I'm not.

                    PETER
          Really?... You'd leave your home?
          Your family? ...Your whole life?

                    VALERIE
          I'll do anything to be with you.

                    PETER
          I thought you'd say that.

Valerie mock-punches him. He grabs her wrist.
Intense.

                    PETER (CONT'D)
          Let's do something about it.

Just then, a horse chuffs—Valerie turns. There
are TWO WORKHORSES visible through the trees.
Unattended.

                    VALERIE
          We'll be half a day's ride before
          anyone even knows we're gone.

                    PETER
          I'll race you.

Valerie runs toward the horses. Peter chases
after her.

EXT. FIELD OF HAYSTACKS - DAY

We're running with Claude now, when suddenly—

—he stops, frozen. His eyes go wide,
HE DROPS THE TAROT CARD, he STUTTERS,
and all he gets out is...

                    CLAUDE
          ... W... W... W...

WE SEE what fills him with fear: A young
woman lies dead in the field.
Her DRESS in tatters, skin CLAWED.

Curious and fearful, Claude can't resist touching
her exposed leg. He pulls back, then runs away.

EXT. VILLAGE - DAY - (PRE-SNOW)

We're racing with Claude through the Village Gate...

As he runs, we see that the village hasn't changed much
from the memory—the fortified homes, the log wall. In a
prosperous blacksmith shop, a handsome FATHER and SON worl
the forge, watching Claude run past.

Claude finally stops before a rustic INN.

                         CLAUDE
          W—W—W—

His mother MARGUERITE charges angrily from the Tavern.

                         MARGUERITE
          I'm working.

Marguerite lunges for Claude as his sister, ROXANNE (17),
runs from the well and gets between them as he says—

                         CLAUDE
          M-m-mama... it's the W-W-Wolf...

EXT. PINE TREE - DAY - (PRE-SNOW)

Peter and Valerie are sprinting toward the horses when the
SUDDEN CLANGING of a Church bell stops her. That sound
means something. SOMETHING BAD.

EXT. FIELD OF HAYSTACKS - DAY - (PRE-SNOW)

The bell CONTINUES TO RING. Valerie runs through the haystacks. Peter follows with several other Villagers.

Neighbors SEE VALERIE AND LOOK AWAY. She runs faster.

Valerie comes upon THREE GIRLS. Claude's sister Roxanne, serious PRUDENCE, and sultry ROSE. The Girls hang on each other, sobbing. Murmuring.

                    ROSE
          It killed again—

                    ROXANNE
          But we've kept the peace!

                    PRUDENCE
          Well, the Wolf has broken it.

                    VALERIE
          Who is it? Tell me...

                    ROXANNE
          Your sister.

Valerie reels—unsteady. Push into her eyes...

Distraught, Valerie sees the Villagers gathered at the field's edge. She walks quickly toward them. They move out of her way, leaving a COUPLE. Isolated.

                    VALERIE
          Mother... Father...?

Her father, CESAIRE (40), was handsome once, but hard labor and drink have taken their toll. Such sorrow in his eyes...

27

Valerie's mother, SUZETTE (40), is a striking woman, completely devastated by grief.

Valerie sees the body of Lucie, sprawled in the hay. Now lifeless.

The hayfield seems to swirl around Valerie. ALL SOUND DRAINS AWAY. She drops to her knees, sobbing. SNOWFLAKES start to fall. As the CAMERA SPIRALS UP AND AWAY...

INT. VALERIE'S COTTAGE - DAY (SNOW FALLS OUTSIDE)

The small cottage is crowded with grieving neighbors.

Valerie's girlfriends (Roxanne, Rose, Prudence) help prepare Lucie's body for burial. Cesaire watches, drinking from a flask. Suzette reaches out to him, but he sadly waves her away. He wants to be alone.

Valerie lights candles, barely choking back tears. Roxanne sees this and kneels at her side.

Roxanne puts a hand on her shoulder. He places a little corn husk angel on the shrine and turns to Valerie, seeking her approval. She smiles, then—

A LOUD KNOCK. Suzette looks through the peephole.

                    SUZETTE
          It's the Lazars.

Suzette shoots Cesaire a disapproving look and hides his flask. Then she quickly tries to tidy Valerie's hair, but Valerie pulls away. Cesaire gives her a sympathetic look, then distracts her mother by opening the bolted door.

Valerie climbs up the ladder, escaping to her sleeping loft. She nods a "Thank you" to her father. We see that they have their own special way of communicating.

IN THE LOFT, Valerie sits on the bed she shared with her sister. Valerie looks over the rail and watches as, BELOW...

Three generations of the wealthiest family in town enter: MADAME LAZAR (65) and the blacksmiths—Madame Lazar's son ADRIEN (40) and her grandson HENRY (21).

Henry is DASHING in a long leather coat. Prudence and Roxanne blush, but Rose greets Henry with a smile.

Henry's eyes scan right by her. He spots Valerie in the loft. She shrinks back. Suzette notices.

28

> MADAME LAZAR
> I am sorry for your loss.

Henry helps Madame Lazar to a chair. Adrien hugs
Suzette, then he hugs Cesaire.

> ADRIEN
> Lucie was a good girl.

IN THE LOFT, Valerie watches with dread as her mother
climbs up the ladder toward her. Whispering.

> SUZETTE
> He's your fiancé now. He wants to offer his
> condolences.

> VALERIE
> I barely even know him.

> SUZETTE
> You'll get to know him.

> VALERIE
> Not now, Mother.

> SUZETTE
> I didn't love your father when we were
> married. I was in love with someone else....
> But I grew to love your father.
> And he gave me two beautiful daughters.
> Now go down there. Please.

DOWN BELOW, Henry sees that Valerie doesn't want to
talk to him, so he speaks loudly to Cesaire.

> HENRY
> Come with us to the tavern. Let the women
> grieve in their own way.

IN THE LOFT, Valerie gives Henry a grateful look as
he and Adrien escort Cesaire toward the door.

EXT. DYE SHOP — AFTERNOON (SNOW FALLING)

A Sheepshearer finishes shaving his ewe, a man
dyeing wool in shallow vats puts down his cloth.
The REEVE (now 50) impatiently tries to usher the
workers out. A rail-thin priest, FATHER AUGUSTE,
tries to calm him.

> THE REEVE
> They're waiting.

Cesaire

Suzette

29

The Reeve stalks off out of the dye shop toward the
Tavern. Father Auguste hot on his trail.

                    FATHER AUGUSTE
          We should count our blessings. It's
          been almost twenty years since the
          Wolf has taken a human life—

INT.   VILLAGE TAVERN - AFTERNOON - (SNOW FALLING OUTSIDE)

All the Men are here. Three dozen of them with their FEAR
and their DRINK. There is discord and panic.

The Reeve and Father Auguste bust through the doors of
the Tavern—still arguing.

We thought that Henry's long leather coat would be a hand-me-down from his father

Xu Stoler

HENRY LAZAR

30

THE REEVE
Because we sacrifice our best livestock
every full moon.

TAVERN OWNER
We kept our end of the bargain.
But now the Wolf feeds on us?!

ADRIEN (O.S.)
SO NOW WE KILL IT.

All eyes go to Adrien, who is entering the Tavern with
Cesaire and Henry. DRUNKEN CHEERS from the Men.

ADRIEN
LAZAR

CESAIRE

INT. VALERIE'S COTTAGE - AFTERNOON - (SNOW FALLING OUTSIDE)

Rose whispers to Prudence and Roxanne.

                    ROSE
          I wonder why she was outside on a
          Wolf night...

                    SUZETTE
          The beast came in and took her.

                    MADAME LAZAR
          And nobody heard anything? In a
          house this small?
                         (to Valerie)
          Don't you sleep in the same bed with her?

                    PRUDENCE
          Maybe she snuck out to meet a boy.

                    SUZETTE
          My Lucie didn't even notice boys.

                    MADAME LAZAR
          She was very taken with my grandson.
          She used to come by and follow him
          around like a puppy. If she found out
          that night that Henry was engaged to
          her sister...

                    ROXANNE
          It must have broken her heart—

                    ROSE
          Maybe she chose to die rather than
          live without him...

                    PRUDENCE
          How romantic.

                    SUZETTE
          It's unthinkable.

Suzette is furious. But Valerie is reeling.
FLASH: *In their bed, Valerie tells Lucie a story.*
Lucie is quiet.

                    VALERIE
          She never told me how she felt...

32   MADAME LAZAR

MADAME LAZAR
(to Valerie)
Don't worry, dear. Henry always had
his eye on you. You're the *pretty* one.

Madame Lazar strokes Valerie's cheek.

INT. VILLAGE TAVERN - AFTERNOON

FATHER AUGUSTE
It's time to ask for help.
(beat)
I've summoned Father Solomon.

MURMURS at the mention of this name.

FATHER AUGUSTE
He's destroyed werewolves and
witches in cities throughout the
kingdom. His warriors hail from
Spain, from the Far East... even a
pair of Moors.
(reverentially)
He'll rid us of this beast.

CESAIRE
He's a priest. He probably bored
them to death.
(drains his mug, turns serious)
No. He'll rob us of our vengeance.

Some of the Men AGREE. Father Auguste speaks gently.

FATHER AUGUSTE
She was your child, but—

ADRIEN
Any of our children could be next.

INT. VALERIE'S COTTAGE - AFTERNOON (SNOW FALLING OUTSIDE)

The Girls have joined Valerie in the loft. Downstairs,
Claude tries a card trick on Madame Lazar. Suzette
pulls Claude away from Madame Lazar and hands him a
coin to quiet him. Then, she hears a NOISE on the porch...

33

EXT. VALERIE'S BALCONY - AFTERNOON - (SNOW FALLING)

Suzette opens the peephole door, startling Peter. He is
placing a gilded saint's candle on the rail.

                    SUZETTE
          Get out of here.

                    PETER
          I'm paying my respects.

                    SUZETTE
          I know why you're here.
                    (stepping outside)
          I've just lost one daughter. Valerie is
          all I have left. You have nothing to
          offer her.

                    PETER
          I have a trade. The same one as your
          husband.

                    SUZETTE
          I know exactly what a woodcutter
          earns. That's why Henry is her only
          hope for a better life.

Peter looks into Suzette's anguished eyes: Her words
strike a chord with Peter's better nature.

                    SUZETTE
          If you really love her, you'll leave
          her alone.

INT. TAVERN - DAY

                    ADRIEN
          We've seen the bones on the trail to
          Mt. Grimmoor. In Black Raven Woods.
          That's where the Wolf makes its lair.
          We all know it. We've just been too
          cowardly to do anything about it. And
          now this man's daughter is dead.

                    THE REEVE
          We've let this go on too long—

                    TAVERN OWNER
        We know the weaknesses of the werewolf:
        It can't come out in daylight—

                    FATHER AUGUSTE
        It can't step onto Holy Ground—

                    THE REEVE
        (unsheathing an old silver knife)
        And there's silver...

                    ADRIEN
        We're hunters. Let's hunt it.

Some MURMURS of agreement. Henry shifts, uneasy...

                    HENRY
        Maybe Father Auguste is right. Maybe we
        should wait...

There's a stifled LAUGH from one of the lofts. Henry looks
up: Peter has entered the Tavern. From their looks, we sense
that Henry and Peter have been rivals their whole lives. Two
young alpha males in a small town, from different sides of
the tracks.

Adrien grabs a drink and shoves it into Henry's hands.

                    ADRIEN
        Maybe, my son, you should find your
        courage.

Embarrassed, Henry screws up his courage.

                    HENRY
        You want to hunt the Wolf. Let's hunt it.

                    PETER
        No. Let's kill that GODDAMN WOLF.

Peter JUMPS down from the ladder. The Reeve POUNDS his mug.
Gung ho. Soon the Tavern is filled with the sound of mugs
RHYTHMICALLY POUNDING ON TABLETOPS and of DRUNKEN CHEERS.

INT. VALERIE'S HOUSE - DAY

Just then, Rose hears something and goes to the peephole.

                    ROSE
        The men are leaving!

36

EXT. TAVERN - CHURCH SQUARE - AFTERNOON (SNOW FALLING)

PETER steps out of the Tavern. The men, drunk and full of swagger, stream out.

They head out of the village, a ragtag militia brandishing their crude weapons. Wives and children spill out of homes and hug their men, crying.

Valerie, distraught, races through the crowd and finds Peter, but when he sees her, his face darkens. He steps into a WOODSHED. Valerie follows.

> VALERIE
> Be careful. I just lost my sister. I
> can't lose you, too.

Valerie takes his hand, but he pulls away, though he's aching to touch her. Her neck, her back...

> PETER
> We can't do this anymore. You have to
> go through with it. You have to marry
> Henry.

> VALERIE
> But you know I don't want him.

Peter looks at Valerie, her green eyes brilliant and passionate. After a beat, he sets his jaw and—

> PETER
> Don't make this something that it's
> not. We had our fun. But that's all it
> ever was.

> VALERIE
> I don't believe you.

Eyes blazing, Peter blasts past her, out of the shed. He rejoins the march, disappearing in the throng. Valerie, shattered, collects herself and exits. She sees Henry walking through the crowd toward her.

> HENRY
> I made something for you. I was going
> to wait until our wedding, but... just
> in case...

He reaches into his pocket and reveals a simple, elegant copper BRACELET. He gently slips it on Valerie's wrist. In spite of her conflicting emotions, Valerie is touched.

> HENRY
> You will be happy again. I promise...

37

There's a hint of sexual confidence in Henry's tone. Valerie watches curiously as he joins the men. There may be something more to him...

A dozen brave men step through the Gate. Soon they are swallowed up by the dark woods...

EXT. DARK FOREST - LATE AFTERNOON (SNOWING)

The men trek through the dreamlike world of these woods. Cesaire strides up next to Adrien.

                    CESAIRE
          Thank you for standing up for Lucie.
          It was no small thing.

                    ADRIEN
          We'll be family soon. You'd have done
          the same.

The two walk on... and we see VALERIE, peering out from behind a tree, tracking the men stealthily through the shadows like a HUNTRESS.

EXT. DARK FOREST - LATE AFTERNOON (SNOWING)

ON VALERIE as she tracks the men. They approach an eccentric TREE HOUSE built around three huge pines. Animal totems are carved into the eaves of the steeply pitched roof. This is GRANDMOTHER'S HOUSE.

Valerie's grandmother steps out and climbs downstairs. She's an exotic beauty, now tearstained, wracked with grief. She embraces Cesaire.

Mother and son comfort each other.

                    GRANDMOTHER
          Promise me you'll be careful.

                    CESAIRE
          Don't worry. The Wolf wouldn't want me—
          I'm all gristle.

Mother looks at her son fondly; he's trying to cheer her up even when he's full of pain. They embrace tightly, then Cesaire disappears into the woods after the men.

EXT. MT. GRIMMOOR - DUSK (SNOWING)

The men climb up MT. GRIMMOOR. A rugged mass of black rock the Devil could call home.

EXT. GRANDMOTHER'S COTTAGE - DUSK (SNOWING)

It is quiet. Sensing something, Grandmother looks into the
woods and sees Valerie step from behind a tree.

                    VALERIE
          Grandmother...

Valerie throws herself into her grandmother's arms.
Grandmother struggles to stay strong for her as Valerie's
tears pour out.

EXT. VILLAGE - DUSK (SNOWING)

Night is approaching. Sheep are locked behind HEAVY DOORS.
LADDERS are drawn up into the stilt houses.

EXT. WOLF TEMPLE SQUARE - DUSK (SNOWING)

The Full Moon sign creaks in the wind. Father Auguste
watches a poor family chain a GOAT to the Altar.

EXT. MT. GRIMMOOR - DUSK (SNOWING)

The men of the village start to ascend the steep path to
the peak.

INT. GRANDMOTHER'S COTTAGE - NIGHT (SNOWING)

Wind whips against the walls, but the cottage is cozy.
Tree trunks come up from the floor. The bedroom is divided
by a silk curtain. A fire blazes in the hearth. Valerie
reads a book of runes. She sits on a cozy couch, a BLACK
CAT asleep on her feet. Flooded with memories.

                    VALERIE
          There were so many things she
          didn't tell me. I'm her sister.
          I should have known.

GRANDMOTHER'S
HOUSE

> GRANDMOTHER
> That was her choice. We all have
> secrets.

Grandmother cuts a thick slice of bread and ladles a stew into a bowl for Valerie, trying to cheer her up.

> GRANDMOTHER
> Remember, my Granny used to say.
> "All sorrows are—

> VALERIE
> —less with bread."

Valerie smiles weakly at their running joke. She takes a bite of stew. *Mmmm...*

Valerie looks out at the frozen woods. SHIVERS. Cold. Sad. Her grandmother sees this and... goes to a HOPE CHEST and pulls something out.

> GRANDMOTHER
> Try this on...

Grandmother takes out a BEAUTIFUL, DEEP-RED HOODED CLOAK. She lays it about Valerie's shoulders, pulls the RED HOOD up around Valerie's head. She is stunning.

> GRANDMOTHER
> I was making it for your wedding.

> VALERIE
> It doesn't feel like *my* wedding. It
> feels like I'm being sold.

Grandmother frowns. Her heart goes out to this girl. A younger version of herself. She takes Valerie's hand.

> GRANDMOTHER
> Oh, Valerie, I wish I could help
> you follow your dreams...

Valerie looks at her grandmother, realizing that she understands her.

Catherine Hardwicke

41

designing THE RED CLOAK

costume designer Cindy Evans used a two-tone crimson
in India. the swirling paisley pattern was embroidered

the fabric hand-dyed
circle of 8 women.

43

EXT. MT. GRIMMOOR - NEAR THE PEAK - NIGHT (SNOWING)

Cold up here, and the men LEAN INTO THE WIND to make
headway. The Reeve reaches the entrance to the CAVE. The men
look at their meager weapons, but the Reeve charges into the
lair, waving his old knife. The others follow, vanishing into
blackness.

INT. CAVE TUNNEL - MT. GRIMMOOR - NIGHT

The Reeve's torchlight reveals two tunnels branching off.

                    THE REEVE
          Split up.

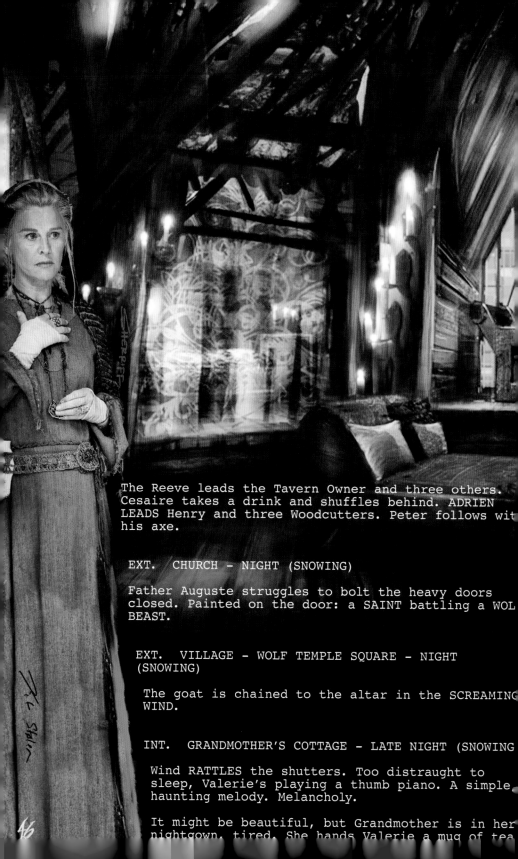

The Reeve leads the Tavern Owner and three others.
Cesaire takes a drink and shuffles behind. ADRIEN
LEADS Henry and three Woodcutters. Peter follows wit
his axe.

EXT. CHURCH - NIGHT (SNOWING)

Father Auguste struggles to bolt the heavy doors
closed. Painted on the door: a SAINT battling a WOL
BEAST.

EXT. VILLAGE - WOLF TEMPLE SQUARE - NIGHT
(SNOWING)

The goat is chained to the altar in the SCREAMING
WIND.

INT. GRANDMOTHER'S COTTAGE - LATE NIGHT (SNOWING

Wind RATTLES the shutters. Too distraught to
sleep, Valerie's playing a thumb piano. A simple,
haunting melody. Melancholy.

It might be beautiful, but Grandmother is in her
nightgown, tired. She hands Valerie a mug of tea

                    GRANDMOTHER
          Drink this. It'll help you sleep.

                    VALERIE
          Is that witchcraft?

                    GRANDMOTHER
          Ooh, yes...
                    (laughing)
          ...it'll turn you into a
          frog.

     Valerie smiles and takes a tentative sip.

                    GRANDMOTHER
          Have a little more.

     Valerie takes another sip, then lays down, her
     heavy eyes gazing into the fire.

INT. CAVE TUNNELS - MT. GRIMMOOR - VARIOUS - NIGHT

Peter, Adrien, Henry, and the Woodcutters come to a fork.
One branch is narrower and more treacherous.

                        PETER
                  (to the woodcutters)
            We'll take the steep one.

                        HENRY
            No. We should stay together—

But Peter, anxious to get away from Henry, is already
climbing down the steep tunnel. The Woodcutters follow him.
Adrien gestures to Henry, who reluctantly follows.

INT. GRANDMOTHER'S COTTAGE - NIGHT (SNOWING)

Valerie is nearly asleep. On the edge of dreams...

                        VALERIE
            ...The Wolf killed Lucie...

INT. CAVE TUNNELS - MT. GRIMMOOR - NIGHT

Adrien and Henry move down the main tunnel. Suddenly,
Henry stops—he hears something.

Adrien continues for a moment, then he looks back at his
son. The wind BLOWS OUT THE TORCH... BLACKNESS.

In ANOTHER TUNNEL, Peter leads his men up the steep
passage, but the WINDS RIPS the FLAME from his torch...
BLACKNESS.

INT. CAVE TUNNEL - MT. GRIMMOOR - NIGHT

The Reeve, with a blazing torch, leads his men down a
winding tunnel. Suddenly, the Reeve stops—they hear a
HORRIBLE SCREAM OF PAIN from another tunnel. It is a man's
scream. A MAN BEING TORTURED. The Reeve starts racing
toward the sound. His men reluctantly follow...

EXT. VILLAGE - WOLF TEMPLE SQUARE - NIGHT (SNOWING)

The chained goat. SUDDENLY, the wind dies. It is stone dead
silent, but for the SMALL BELL on the goat's neck.

INT. CAVE TUNNEL - MT. GRIMMOOR - NIGHT

The WIND IS GONE HERE, too. THE ONLY SOUNDS are the
terrified breathing and fast footsteps of MEN RUNNING
IN FEAR.

The Reeve is up front, sweaty and pale, but charging bravely
toward the screams. As he runs down the dark tunnel, the
screams dissolve into a low moan...

LAIR OF THE WOLF

7A

Unfortunately, the real wolf didn't want t

INT.   CAVERNOUS CHAMBER - MT. GRIMMOOR - NIGHT

The Reeve races in. There's no moaning anymore. He waves his
torch and sees a tower made of wood and HUMAN BONES. The Reeve
turns away, horrified. His men have trickled into the cavern,
watching from the entrance. The Reeve steps deeper into the
cavern, and SEES...

ADRIEN, propped against a rock, the ground beneath him wet with
dark blood. As the Reeve stares at the dead man, he hears A LOW
GROWL. The Reeve spins and sees...

A SNARLING GRAY WOLF.

The Reeve holds out his silver knife with a shaking hand. The
wolf GROWLS, baring teeth. Then THE WOLF LUNGES—

—AND SMASH CUT TO—

INT.   GRANDMOTHER'S COTTAGE - DAWN

BANG! Valerie startles awake. She's fallen asleep on the couch
by the fire. She looks around...

The silk veil to the bedchamber ripples. A slight breeze is
blowing it. Or is it a person?

Valerie opens the veil.

VALERIE'S POV: Grandmother sleeps UNDER THE COVERS, turned away
from Valerie. Or at least it looks like her. We don't see her
face, just a shape in the bed.

Suddenly, THE SHAPE RISES UP FROM THE BED.

Valerie GASPS.

It's GRANDMOTHER... she's groggy,
but smiling.

                    GRANDMOTHER
          Good morning, dear.

Valerie breathes a sigh of relief. Smiles weakly.

EXT.   THE FOREST - DAWN (SNOW COVERED)

In her RED CLOAK, Valerie runs swiftly through the trees, a
flash of color in a snowy white world...

*the trainer had to
give the wolf a
big hunk of meat,
then pull it away
from him to get him
to look VICIOUS!*

52

EXT.   VILLAGE - WOLF TEMPLE SQUARE - DAY (SNOW COVERED)

Valerie slips into the village. She stops. The village
seems DESERTED. She hears sounds coming from the Tavern.
She approaches...

INT.   TAVERN - DAY

Valerie steps inside. EVERYONE IS HERE. There is drink,
joy, and laughter. The Reeve sits at the bar with the
SEVERED WOLF'S HEAD.

Valerie SEES Cesaire and her girlfriends. Everyone is lit
up with DRINK. Across the room, SHE SEES PETER. Relief
floods her face. He is longing to talk to her...

Then she notices that everyone turns toward the window.
It's CLAUDE, with his nose pressed up against the glass.
Smiling. Goofy.

But now Claude is startled. He ducks away as...

The UNDERTAKER'S CART travels past, carrying Adrien's body.
Madame Lazar follows, wailing in grief.

The old woman looks RIGHT INSIDE AT VALERIE. Startling her.
Then Cesaire stands, raises his mug, and calls out.

                    CESAIRE
          To Adrien. For his sacrifice.

INT. BLACKSMITH'S SHOP - DAY

Valerie enters the shop. Her POV: Henry hammers a RED-HOT
HINGE, his back toward her. Valerie watches him working
out his raw pain in the fire. She takes a deep breath, and
softly says—

                    VALERIE
          Your father was a brave man.

Her words strike a nerve. Henry explodes.

                    HENRY
          I was close enough to smell it. But I
          was afraid. I hid from it. I should have
          done something. I should have saved him.

Henry pounds recklessly on the hot anvil.

                              VALERIE
                 Henry... I've lost someone, too. Please come
                 away from the fire.

He keeps pounding. Sparks flying. Valerie steps closer.

                              VALERIE
                 Henry, turn around.

He doesn't. He just pounds harder. His dark shape is twisted
and made beastly by the shadows from the fire. Valerie shivers.
She takes another step, nervous now...

                              HENRY
                 Leave, Valerie. I don't want you to see me
                 like this.

BLAM! BLAM! He strikes the anvil over and over. Flames ripple
the air. Henry does not look like himself. Shaken, Valerie
turns and hurries out the door—

EXT. VILLAGE – BLACKSMITH'S HOUSE/SHOP – DAY (G.S. SHOT)

—and sees Suzette. Teary eyed, her mother stares in the
Lazars's window at Adrien, wrapped in a shroud. Valerie is
stunned: She sees the depth of her mother's grief. Adrien was
obviously more than just a neighbor...

Suzette looks at Valerie—her secret is out. Suzette rushes
away, passing excited Villagers spilling out of the Tavern,
carrying the wolf's head on a pike. Valerie catches up with her
mother, putting the pieces together.

                              VALERIE
                 It was Henry's father, wasn't it? The man
                 you loved?

Suzette walks faster, passing two carpenters starting to build
a Wolf Effigy. Valerie quickens her pace, too.

                              VALERIE
                 Lucie was in love with Henry. She was a
                 year older than me. She could have married
                 him and brought wealth to our family. Why
                 did you insist that it was me?

Suzette turns away. She can barely choke out the words.

                              SUZETTE
                 I think you know the answer.

                              VALERIE
                 I want you to say it.

Suzette is tearful.

                    SUZETTE
          Lucie was Henry's half-sister. She was not
          your father's daughter.

Valerie suddenly looks ill. Almost repulsed by her mother's
secret. WHIP PAN over to CESAIRE across the street, helping
build the effigy. Reluctant, she asks:

                    VALERIE
          Am I his daughter?

                    SUZETTE
          Yes.

                    VALERIE
          Does Papa know about Lucie?

                    SUZETTE
          No. Promise me you won't tell him.

But she is interrupted by the POUNDING of HORSE HOOVES.
Valerie, Suzette, and the Villagers turn to the Main Gate.
FATHER AUGUSTE rushes out into the square, smoothing his
hair. He can barely contain his delight.

                    FATHER AUGUSTE
          He's here.

EXT. VILLAGE - NEAR CHURCH SQUARE - DAY

HOOVES THUNDER across the snow. Massive wooden coach wheels
RUMBLE, relentless. WEAPONS gleam.

The entire village witnesses the arrival of SIX SOLDIERS,
riding through the Main Gate atop POWERFUL STALLIONS. Valerie
sees a Spaniard with a gleaming TIZONA SWORD, a Japanese man
with a KUSARIGAMA, and other fierce-looking armed men. The
Soldiers ride escort to a STAFF COACH.

A MASKED BOWMAN rides on a MASSIVE WHITE STEED, wearing a
fearsome helmet, a WICKED-LOOKING CROSSBOW on his back.

Behind this coach, an additional SIX SOLDIERS march beside
a cart with a HUGE BRONZE ELEPHANT on it. Claude runs along
next to it. He reaches out and strokes the Elephant's trunk.

The caravan stops in the square. A pair of Soldiers dismount
and remove their helmets: They are BROTHERS—the magnificent
Moors. Coiled bullwhips hang from their belts. The Villagers
are astonished.

The younger brother places a stool in front of the STAFF
COACH. The older brother, the CAPTAIN, opens the door.

Everyone holds their breath as a striking man with gentle
blue eyes emerges from the coach. He wears a deep PURPLE
PRIESTLY ROBE. A heavy IRON CROSS. LEATHER GLOVES. His
hair is swept back like Bono. Powerful, confident, but also
warm, gracious.

This is FATHER SOLOMON. He smiles at the crowd, then he
turns and leans back into the coach.

TWO LITTLE GIRLS inside sit next to a proper-looking
woman, their GUARDIAN. Beautiful and sad, the Girls look at
Solomon, sniffling. Solomon looks at them tenderly...

                    SOLOMON
          Now, please don't cry. See all these
          children? See how scared they are?...
          There is a big, bad Wolf here. Someone
          has to stop it.
                    LITTLE GIRL
          Is it the beast that killed our mother?

                    SOLOMON
          It may very well be.

He holds out his arms. They hug him, he kisses each of them
on the head, then SADLY NODS to their Guardian: It's time.
The Guardian pulls the Girls away.

Solomon hardens himself against their tears and closes the
coach door.

The Driver pulls out, escorted by TWO SOLDIERS. Solomon
sees his children looking back at him from the coach's rear
window. He wishes he could go with them, but he hears—

                    FATHER AUGUSTE (O.S.)
          This is indeed an honor, Your Eminence.

Solomon's face changes. The love drains away. He readies
himself for work.

Solomon shakes hands with Father Auguste. He eyes the
effigy, the decorations, the severed wolf's head. The Reeve
proudly steps forward.

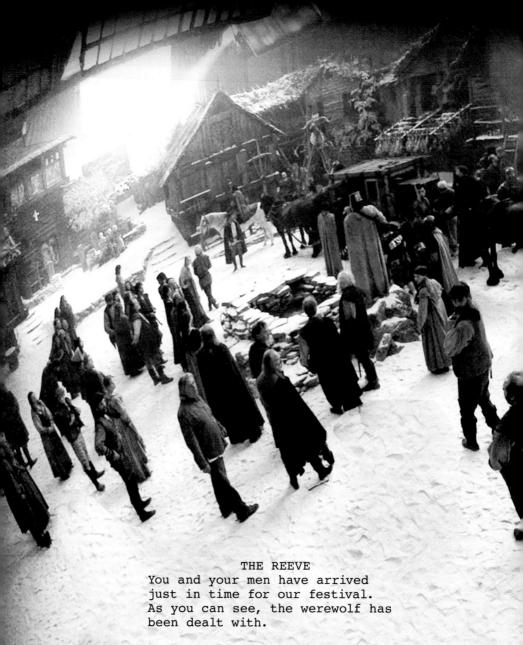

THE REEVE
You and your men have arrived
just in time for our festival.
As you can see, the werewolf has
been dealt with.

SOLOMON
That's not the head of a
werewolf.

THE REEVE
No disrespect, but we've
lived with this beast for two
generations. Every full moon, it
takes our sacrifice. We know what
we're dealing with.

SOLOMON
No disrespect, but you have no
idea what you're dealing with.
(beat)
I was the same way once. My wife's
name was Pénélope. She gave me
two beautiful daughters. We were a
very happy family.

PRESENTING HIS EMINENCE...

FATHER SOLOMON

SOLOMON (CONT'D)
We lived in a village like this.
And like Daggörhorn, ours was
plagued by a werewolf. One full
moon, my friends and I got drunk.
We decided to hunt it. It never
even occurred to us that we might
actually find it. But we did.
            (beat)
I hacked at it with my axe, and
suddenly it was gone. I had cut
off one of its front paws. I
thought it would make a clever
souvenir, and so I took it home.
            (beat)
There, I found my wife with a
bloody rag tied around her left
wrist. And when I opened my sack,
the werewolf's paw was gone. This
was in its place.

Solomon nods to his Captain, who
produces a wooden box. He opens the
lid... Children peek into the box. They
scream and run away, then sneak back
for another look.

SOLOMON (CONT'D)
I told my girls that the werewolf
killed their mother. But that was a
lie. I killed her.

63

Solomon turns and gives the Reeve a hard look.

>   SOLOMON
>   When a werewolf dies, it returns to its
>   human form.
>   (re: wolf head)
>   That's just a common gray wolf. Your
>   werewolf is still alive.

But the Reeve isn't buying it. He and the other Villagers
grumble in disagreement as...

INT.   VILLAGE TAVERN - DAY

The Reeve and other Villagers follow Solomon inside. He
motions to his Soldiers to unload their gear. They carry
crates of weapons and instruments: medical, astronomical,
scientific. A Soldier/Scribe takes notes in a leather-bound
ledger.

Solomon unsheathes his SWORD. The silver blade GLEAMS.
The gem-encrusted hilt depicts Christ on the cross. Father
Auguste's eyes light up like a fanboy's.

>   FATHER AUGUSTE
>   This is one of only three silver swords
>   blessed by the Holy See. May I touch—

>   SOLOMON
>   No. This is a very dangerous time.
>   You all know what the Blood Moon
>   means.
>   (off blank stares)
>   You have no idea what it means.

64

My wife's name was Pénélope...

AD MAJOREM D

...AY I TOUCH IT?

THE ORRERY

The Reeve tries to cover his ignorance. Solomon isn't buying it. He nods to the Captain.

The Soldiers open a large trunk, carefully remove a brass device, and set it on the table. It's a three-dimensional representation of a medieval solar system.

CAPTAIN

The orrery.

Solomon adjusts the positions of Mars and the moon.

SOLOMON
The red planet converges with the
moon once every thirteen years...

He lights a candle, creating a magical red glow behind
the glass orbs. The Villagers are fascinated.

SOLOMON
This is the ONLY TIME A NEW WEREWOLF

Surprised, Valerie and the Villagers murmur.

                    SOLOMON
          During the week of the Blood Moon,
          the werewolf may pass his curse
          on with a single bite. Even in
          daytime—

                    THE REEVE
          You're wrong. Sunlight makes a
          werewolf human—

                    SOLOMON
          No, you're wrong. A werewolf is
          never truly human.

                    CAPTAIN
          During a normal full moon, a wolf
          bite will kill you. But during a
          Blood Moon, your very *souls* are in
          danger.

The room is dead quiet. Chilled.

                    SOLOMON
          Until the Blood Moon wanes in three
          days, you will never truly be safe.

                    THE REEVE
          We're safe now. I killed the wolf.
          In its lair—

                    TAVERN OWNER
          The cave at Mt. Grimmoor.

Jupiter

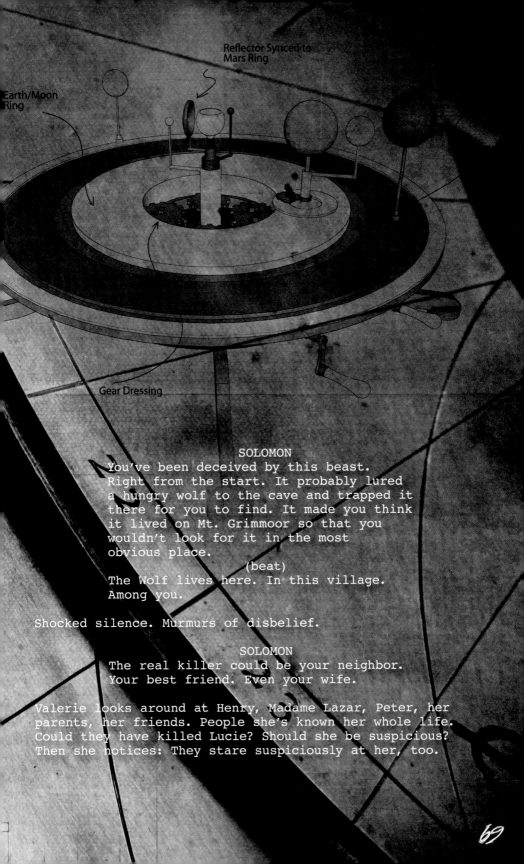

Reflector Synced to
Mars Ring

Earth/Moon
Ring

Gear Dressing

SOLOMON
You've been deceived by this beast.
Right from the start. It probably lured
a hungry wolf to the cave and trapped it
there for you to find. It made you think
it lived on Mt. Grimmoor so that you
wouldn't look for it in the most
obvious place.
                    (beat)
The Wolf lives here. In this village.
Among you.

Shocked silence. Murmurs of disbelief.

SOLOMON
The real killer could be your neighbor.
Your best friend. Even your wife.

Valerie looks around at Henry, Madame Lazar, Peter, her
parents, her friends. People she's known her whole life.
Could they have killed Lucie? Should she be suspicious?
Then she notices: They stare suspiciously at her, too.

Solomon turns to the Captain.

> SOLOMON
> Barricade the village. Post men at every
> gate. No one leaves until we kill the wolf.

The Reeve looks outside: The festival preparations are in full swing. He steps right up to Solomon.

> THE REEVE
> The Wolf is dead. Tonight we celebrate.

The Tavern Owner murmurs his support. Solomon looks at the town leaders. Legendary werewolf hunter or not, he is a stranger here. He considers for a beat. Then:

                    SOLOMON
          Go ahead and celebrate. We'll see who's
          right.

The Reeve smiles, confident. The sound of a LOUD HORN—

EXT. VILLAGE - CHURCH SQUARE - NIGHT

— carries us over to the festival. In the sky: A BLOOD-RED
FULL MOON. In the Church Tower, a drunken WOODCUTTER blows a
CONCH SHELL, then a REVELER in a SHEEP MASK drunkenly slides
down the bell rope and dances past...

A crowd of Villagers, including Henry, Peter, Father
Auguste, and two little old BAKERY LADIES toast the REEVE
in front of the burning WOLF EFFIGY. The SHEEP REVELER
stumbles in front of a makeshift STAGE by the well, where
MUSICIANS play huge horns, drums, and a hurdy-gurdy. A
WOMAN in a CORN HARVEST MASK sings. The Sheep Reveler
grabs a flask and pulls off his mask to drink—it's CESAIRE.

THREE LITTLE PIGS dance past. A MAN IN A WOLF COSTUME
huffs and puffs and "blows" them down. A GIRL spins balls
of fire. This village needed a PARTY...

There's no sign of Solomon or his men.

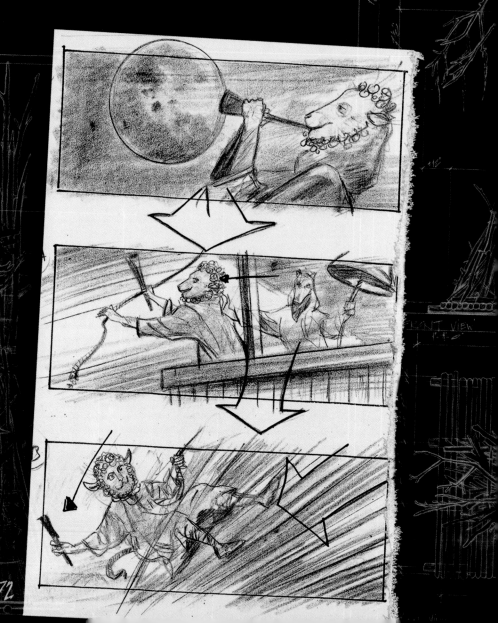

LIFTS MASK — CESAIRE

CESAIR PICKS-UP BOTTLE —

NEAR THE EFFIGY, Father Auguste weaves through the crowd.
Marguerite playfully slaps his ass. He panics and heads
toward the Church.

NEAR THE LAZAR HOUSE, Madame Lazar watches from her second
floor window...

AT THE CHURCH, Father Auguste steps inside and pulls the
doors nearly closed. He peers out the crack...

We made all the instruments from
Heironymous Bosch's painting "The Garden of Earthly Delights."
The tall standing horns, the blue drums, and the Hurdy Gurdy.

75

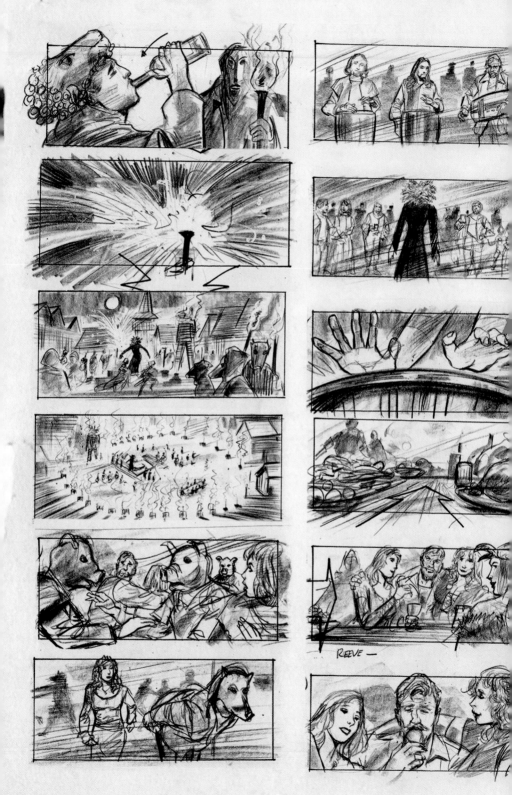

REEVE

76

SMILES

THE FESTIVAL

Preoccupied, Valerie watches Rose, Prudence, Roxanne, and Claude dance.

Suddenly, there's a burst of LAUGHTER. Valerie turns. Her father has passed out drunk in a pool of vomit. The Man in a Wolf Costume is pretending to hump him.

> MAN IN A WOLF COSTUME
> I'll huff and I'll puff and I'll—

IN A FLASH, Valerie GRABS a firewood log and WHACKS the Man to the ground. Villagers step back, impressed. Cesaire stands up and looks at his soiled shirt. He tries to joke.

> CESAIRE
> I'll just flick this off and be fit to
> see the Pope.

> VALERIE
> Papa.

But Valerie isn't laughing. His "loveable drunk" shtick isn't working tonight. Crushed, Cesaire's fragile emotions shift instantly. He tears up.

78

                    CESAIRE
           You're my good girl. I'm so sorry...

Valerie wraps an arm around him.

                    VALERIE
           It's OK... Now go home.

He nods, ashamed. She tenderly but firmly steers him
toward their cottage. When he disappears from sight,
Valerie joins Prudence. Prudence changes the subject.

                    PRUDENCE
           Looks like Rose has a new conquest.

Valerie looks through the crowd: She sees Rose dirty
dancing with Peter. Whoa.

Valerie grabs a MUG OF ALE from a passing reveler and
GULPS IT DOWN. Prudence watches in shock. The drink goes
right to Valerie's head.

Choreographer Sarah Elgart
twisted traditional steps into
a sensual modern dance.

79

EXT. VILLAGE - MAIN GATE - NIGHT

The CELEBRATION MUSIC can be heard in the distance. THE
VILLAGE IS LOCKED DOWN: Bolas Man stands watch from the
Granary Tower; Kusa Man and Sabre Man patrol the dark
tree line.

A Tall Soldier checks on a Young Soldier as he guards the
Main Gate. Claude wanders up and stares at him. The Young
Soldier shifts. Claude reaches out a hand. Nervous, the
Young Soldier flinches... but Claude "snatches" a card from
the Soldier's ear. He smiles. Gotcha. The Young Soldier
laughs. Not bad.

In the shadows, Solomon watches. He steps up to Claude.

                    SOLOMON
          Impressive. Where did you learn that?

Claude just smiles at Solomon. But Roxanne rushes up and
takes her brother's hand, pulling him away.

                    ROXANNE
          Come back to the party, Claude.

EXT. VILLAGE - CHURCH SQUARE - NIGHT

The drummers pound furiously—it's a raucous medieval jam
session. Valerie grabs Prudence and dances with her. Wild,
drawing attention, pretending not to watch Rose booty-grind
up on Peter. Valerie and Peter try WAY TOO HARD not to look
at each other.

Just then, Henry stumbles toward Valerie with an ale, clearly
the latest of many. He follows her look and sees that she's
watching Peter. Henry glares at him... then PUSHES his way
toward Peter and GRABS his shoulder.

                    HENRY
          You left us.

80

Peter is surprised but ready to laugh it off.

                    PETER
          Take it easy, friend.

                    HENRY
          You left us. In the caves.

Peter's smile fades. Henry's pain has turned to fury. Valerie
has seen this before. She rushes to pull him away, but he's
NOT BACKING DOWN.

                    HENRY
          I said we should stick together. But you
          left us. And my father's dead because of
          it.

                    VALERIE
          Please, don't do this—

Henry brushes her aside, but pushes too hard, and she
stumbles. Peter's eyes FLASH IN ANGER. He instantly grabs
Henry's arm. Henry overreacts and PUNCHES him. Peter falls
on his ass. The Villagers laugh.

Peter stands—he has a KNIFE in his hand. He thrusts toward
Henry. Glaring at him.

                    PETER
          You keep your hands off her. Or I'll cut
          them off.

Henry glares back at him. If he's afraid, he doesn't show it.
It's a standoff until...

                    VALERIE (O.S.)
          Peter, don't.

Her voice snaps Peter back to reality. He realizes he's about
to take this too far. He leaves. Valerie hurries after Peter.
Henry watches her go...

EXT. VILLAGE - ALLEYWAY - NEAR WOLF TEMPLE SQUARE - NIGHT

Valerie chases Peter down an alleyway.

                    PETER
Leave me alone. What's the matter with you? What do I have
to do to make you stop?

                    VALERIE
          Peter, I love you.

She's brave with the drink. Peter falters. Valerie's never
said this to him before. She realizes something...

                    VALERIE
          And what the hell are you doing with
          Rose? You don't even like her.

                    PETER
          I don't have to like her to get what I
          want from her.

                    VALERIE
          You're a terrible liar. I know you feel
          like I do.

He fiercely grabs the bracelet Henry gave her.

                    PETER
          I'll never be able to give you anything
          like this.

                    VALERIE
          You think I care about Henry's money?

                    PETER
          You have a future with him. I'm not
          going to let you ruin that.

                    VALERIE
          Did my mother get to you?

                    PETER
          Valerie. I'm wrong for you.

                    VALERIE
          I don't care.

Valerie suddenly kisses him full on the lips, charged and
passionate. He starts to push her away, but she looks up at
him. DARING HIM. Resistance is futile—

He pushes her up against the wall and they kiss, long and hard, their imprisoned feelings BURSTING FREE.

                         PETER
              I could eat you up...

Peter SWEEPS HER UP and CARRIES HER inside the nearby Granary Tower.

INT.   GRANARY TOWER - NEAR WOLF TEMPLE SQUARE - NIGHT

UNKNOWN POV: Someone is WATCHING as Peter lowers Valerie onto a pile of hay. She gasps.

UNKNOWN POV darts behind a post as Valerie turns toward the Watcher... Slowly, the WATCHER edges out from the post and sees Peter kissing Valerie's neck. She responds—twisting, arching her back. He moves against her, breath quickening. She guides his hand to her breast. He hesitates.

                         VALERIE
              Don't you want me?

Peter answers by UNLACING HER BLOUSE. They can't keep their hands off each other—seeking each other's souls—the CAMERA drifts away—

—and FINDS THE WATCHER in the shadows. It is Henry. He studies the lovers. At first, he is FASCINATED, but his feelings quickly turn to RAGE. He is about to step forward when—

Two Woodcutters stumble up the windmill. Henry steps behind the doorway, out of sight.

PETER quickly pulls Valerie to her feet and sneaks her into the shadows, but the Woodcutters see him.

                            WOODCUTTER
                   Peter. Give us a hand.

The Woodcutters start loading a keg. Peter goes upstairs
to help the men. No one notices Henry, watching from
behind the shaft...

PUSH IN ON Henry's EYES... burning. He saw it all...

EXT. MAIN GATE - NIGHT

The Young Soldier patrols the Main Gate. Nervous, alert.
Suddenly, in the shadowy woods behind him, a DARK SHAPE
blurs past and we SMASH CUT to—

EXT. VILLAGE - CHURCH SQUARE - NIGHT

The music is pounding—teenagers race across glowing coals
in their bare feet. Claude stares at Valerie—

She joins the crowd next to Roxanne, who is cheering for
the fire-walkers. Valerie KICKS OFF her boots, then GRABS
a pair of GOAT HORNS from a dancer, ties them around her
head, and RUNS ACROSS THE COALS. Wild. Free. Magnificent
against the roaring flames.

Roxanne then kicks off her shoes and chases Valerie across
the coals, screaming with laughter.

EXT. MAIN GATE - NIGHT

The Tall Soldier rounds a corner and approaches the Main
Gate. He is startled to see a sword lying on the ground,
then steps behind a wagon and sees the Young Soldier lying
on the ground.

EXT. VILLAGE - CHURCH SQUARE - NIGHT

Valerie and Roxanne put on their boots. Valerie scans the
crowd. Her POV: Prudence and Rose sit at the Reeve's table.
ROXANNE notices Valerie's preoccupation.

                    ROXANNE
          Where *did* you disappear to?

Valerie looks at her best friend. She starts to spill...

                    VALERIE
          You know all that soft hay in the
          granary...

But Valerie can't finish her sentence. A couple dances past
her, revealing two GLOWING EYES ACROSS THE SQUARE.

Then... a low, unearthly GROWL. The Villagers gasp. The Musicians' notes twist into horrible distorted sounds. The CHURCH BELL RINGS. Valerie stares at Roxanne.

The eyes RUSH FORWARD—an enormous JET-BLACK BEAST RUSHES across the square and CHARGES at the REEVE.

It's THE WOLF. Its silhouette is a MONSTROUS DARK BLUR. So big it makes the wolf in the cave look like a Chihuahua. Its fur is so black that all we see are its GLARING YELLOW EYES.

The Reeve stands up bravely, drawing his knife.

—IN A RUSH, THE WOLF LUNGES at the REEVE.

THERE'S A BLOOD-CURDLING SCREAM... and the REEVE'S BODY
SMASHES into the big wooden bench. DEAD.

Suddenly, SOLDIERS step out of hiding places scattered
throughout the village. The Captain bursts out onto the
CAPTAIN'S BALCONY and runs downstairs, yelling:

> CAPTAIN
> Get to the church! The Wolf can't
> cross onto holy ground!

Villagers flee in a blind panic. In the chaos, Valerie and
Roxanne follow Claude—heading toward the Rectory.

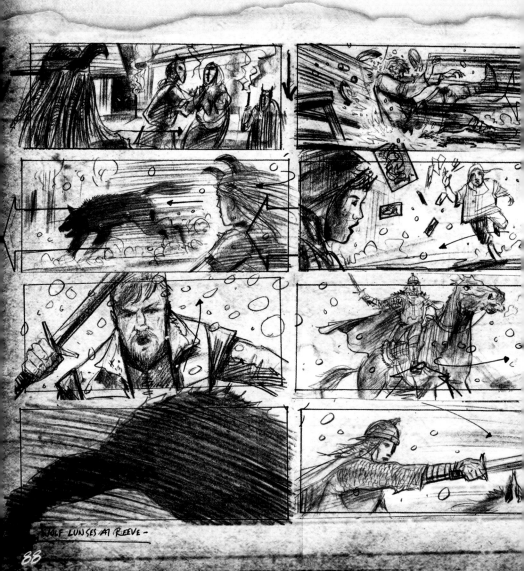

WOLF LUNGES AT REEVE —

                    ROXANNE
          Claude!

Valerie and Roxanne flee, hearts pounding—as a few
lengths behind them, Solomon gallops in under the Tavern
Bridge on the magnificent white steed. Tizona Man jumps
down from a balcony as Solomon gallops past, drawing his
sword and pointing it at the Wolf, SILVER gleaming in the
moonlight. Confident.

                    SOLOMON
          You will die now, beast!

Tizona Man charges forward and swings his sword. The Wolf
dodges it. Sabre Man throws a silver-tipped dagger at the
Wolf. With quick animal reflexes, the Wolf leaps out of
the way.

IN THE RECTORY ALLEY, Valerie and Roxanne get a glimpse of Claude, darting behind the Rectory.

Sabre Man jump down from a BALCONY and tries to save the Fire-Spinning Girl.

SABRE MAN SWINGS fiercely, but the Wolf ducks his blow—then POUNCES ON HIM. In a BLUR of MOTION, the Wolf FLINGS Sabre Man into the LEATHER SHOP drying racks. Dead.

THE WOLF chases the Fire-Spinning Girl past the EFFIGY toward the GLASS SHOP. KILLS HER.

ON THE TAVERN BRIDGE: Valerie and Roxanne look for Claude. They duck behind the railing, watching as:

SOLOMON gestures to his Captain. The Captain and his Brother unfurl silver BULLWHIPS. The Brother CRACKS his whip, snaring the Wolf by a paw. Then—

CRACK! The Captain SNARES the Wolf around the neck. They step back and the whips go taut with the Wolf caught, strangled, between them. Lance Man heads toward the Wolf, ready to finish it off. Solomon smiles.

Suddenly, the Captain and his Brother are DRAGGED through the snow and—the Wolf REARS UP and WHIPS ITS HEAD AROUND WITH A FORCE SO POWERFUL that it sends the Brother FLYING THROUGH THE AIR—SMASHING INTO TIZONA MAN. The Captain is FLUNG ONTO THE GLASS SHOP ROOF.

ON THE TAVERN BRIDGE: Valerie and Roxanne hide behind the railing, watching:

THE BROTHER reaches for his weapon—the Wolf LUNGES at the Brother, snapping his jaws, when Lance Man flings his Lance— the WOLF dodges it, teeth GRAZING the Brother's arm—then the Wolf spins on the Scribe. A BLUR WIPES FRAME—and the Scribe is DEAD. His ledger flung into the snow.

Uncertainty crosses Solomon's face. This is not going according to plan. We see shock. Admiration. And a hint of fear.

ON THE TAVERN BRIDGE—Valerie and Roxanne see...

LANCE MAN running back to Solomon. His face registers more than a hint of fear.

                    LANCE MAN
          It's... strong.

                    SOLOMON
          Have faith. God is stronger.

SOLOMON'S POV: CLOSE ON THE WOLF'S YELLOW EYES.

SOLOMON SNAPS the reins and SPURS his steed to action, rushing right at the Wolf.

Andy Cheng, 2nd Unit Director/Stunt Co-ordinator, worked with Horse Wrangler Danny Virtue, to stage the Wolf Attack.

O.T.S. THE WOLF'S SHOULDER: The Wolf holds his ground.
FEARLESS. CHALLENGING. PURE EVIL.

TIGHT ON THE WOLF'S MOUTH as it growls—an unearthly
sound—Solomon's horse REARS UP, spooked—Solomon FLIES
OFF—and lands in the hot coals.

The Masked Bowman runs into the square and OPENS FIRE
with his crossbow...

...and we realize this is a REPEATING SIEGE CROSSBOW. A
Chinese lever-operated *chu-ko-nu*, spitting silver-tipped
bolts. He FIRES and the Wolf races away—dodging the bolt—
just as KUSA MAN races out from the RECTORY ALLEY and
SWINGS his chain, the DEADLY SILVER BALL arcing toward
the Wolf.

The Wolf LEAPS ATOP the GLASS SHOP, a DARK SHADOW
bounding across the rooftops.

Valerie and Roxanne step out onto a balcony and see:

NEAR THE EFFIGY: In the aftermath, a figure emerges from
the smoke... SOLOMON. He gets to his feet, rising from
the burning coals, brushing hot cinders off his face. His
hair is singed. But he has his sword in hand. He's still
ready to fight, his pain merely galvanizing his resolve.
He yells up to Villagers hiding in their homes.

                    SOLOMON
          I warned you—your werewolf is still
          alive.

He turns to Kusa Man and Lance Man.

                    SOLOMON
          FIND HIM!

NEAR THE EFFIGY: Solomon catches a glimpse of a SHADOWY
FIGURE darting through an ALLEY. He and the Masked
Bowman race after it.

ON THE BALCONY: Valerie and Roxanne hear something BIG
LAND ON THE ROOF ABOVE THEM. Dust falls through the
shingles. Terrified, they scramble downstairs and race
into the DYE SHOP.

Propmaster Dan Sissons based the Masked Bowman's crossbow
on the CHU-KO-NU, a Mongolian repeating crossbow.

EXT. VILLAGE - VARIOUS - NIGHT

UNKNOWN POV from the CAPTAIN'S BALCONY: <u>Someone is</u>
<u>following Valerie and Roxanne</u> as they head downstairs.

BACK TO THE GIRLS—UNKNOWN POV: The STALKER follows close
behind the girls as they duck into the DYE SHOP ALLEY.
They hear a strange CLATTER on the stairs behind them.
Roxanne almost trips.

Valerie grabs her wrist, pulling her back from a vat of
blue dye, shimmering in the moonlight. Suddenly, there's
a low GROWL behind them. The girls whirl around.

<u>They are facing the STALKER. IT IS THE WOLF. ON THE</u>
BRIDGE ABOVE. Roxanne SCREAMS. They look for a way out—

EXT. VILLAGE - DYE SHOP ALLEY - NIGHT

—but the gate is shut and the alley is blocked by wagons
and storage towers of blue flower petals.

The Wolf closes in fast, SPLASHING through the dye vats.
Roxanne and Valerie are TRAPPED in the dead-end alley by
the ENORMOUS BEAST. <u>This is the first time we actually see
the beast.</u> His coal-black matted fur, the huge ears. Made
even more formidable by the doubling of his reflection in
the dye pool.

THE GIRLS ARE TERRIFIED.

Then, inexplicably, ***the Wolf speaks.*** CAMERA MOVES IN TIGHT
on its blazing, mesmerizing eyes, so we don't see its
mouth. We just hear its voice. The devil's voice: an eerie
mix of male, female, human, and animal.

                    THE WOLF
        Did you think you were faster than me?

It looms toward them. TERRIFYING. RAVENOUS. It SNARLS,
showing razor-sharp teeth caked with blood. Glowing even
redder under the crimson moon. VALERIE IS HORRIFIED.

                    VALERIE
          Oh, my God... You speak. How?

                    THE WOLF
          All that matters is that you
          understand me, Valerie.

                    VALERIE
          You know my name—

Roxanne gives her a frightened look.

                    ROXANNE
               (trembling, to Valerie)
          W-what are you doing?

The Wolf WHIRLS on Roxanne and GROWLS, silencing her. It
turns back to Valerie, stepping closer. Valerie recoils.

secrets...

FLASH: *Young Valerie stands under the Pine next to Young Peter. She proudly holds the BLOODY KNIFE in one hand and the DEAD RABBIT in the other.*

                    THE WOLF
          What happened to the rabbit, Valerie?

                    VALERIE
          I killed it.

What happened
to the rabbit,
Valerie?

Valerie's eyes flash at the Memory, recognizing a hint of truth in the Wolf's words. The Wolf sniffs at her feet.

> THE WOLF
> You're a hunter. I can smell it on you even now.

The Wolf sniffs Valerie, its muzzle only inches from her face. Valerie looks into its huge, horrible eyes.

> VALERIE
> What... big... eyes... you... have...

> THE WOLF
> The better to see you with, my dear.

Then suddenly, <u>the skin on either side of the Wolf's brow separates, snapping open to reveal a SECOND PAIR OF EYES.</u> Not yellow ones, but dark brown ones.

> VALERIE
> Human eyes... dark brown...

> THE WOLF
> That's right... You know me well, Valerie.

The Wolf's four mesmerizing eyes fill Valerie's vision...

> THE WOLF
> I know what lies in your heart—you want to escape from this village... you want freedom... to follow your heart...

> VALERIE
> ...no...

> The WOLF
> Come away with me right now...

VISUAL FX SUPERVISOR JEFF OKUN WORKS WITH THE RHYTHM & HUES TEAM TO BRING THE WOLF TO LIFE

Wolf Front View v7.02a   R&H 08.04.2010

Valerie is petrified... Then she hears the CLAMOR of Soldiers. *If she can stall for just a moment...*

> VALERIE
> Father Solomon will stop you.

> THE WOLF
> Father Solomon doesn't know what
> he's dealing with...

The Wolf glances toward the approaching Soldiers. Frustrated. Out of desperation, he threatens her...

> THE WOLF
> Come away with me, or I'll kill
> everyone you love. Starting with
> her.

The Wolf whirls toward Roxanne—his jaws SNAP OPEN. Roxanne is literally SHAKING WITH FEAR.

Valerie is shocked: *How could she make this kind of a choice?* She looks at Roxanne's terror-stricken face as—

—Solomon and the Masked Bowman turn the corner. The Wolf GROWLS at Valerie—

> THE WOLF
> I'll return for you. Before the
> Blood Moon wanes.

Valerie is chilled. The Wolf leaps past her and over the gate as the Masked Bowman raises his crossbow and pulls the trigger. The Wolf disappears as the bolt FIRES into the empty night. Solomon seethes.

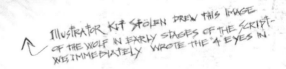

ILLUSTRATOR KIT STÖLEN DREW THIS IMAGE OF THE WOLF IN EARLY STAGES OF THE SCRIPT— WE IMMEDIATELY WROTE THE "4" EYES IN

EXT.   CHURCH - NIGHT

Solomon and the Masked Bowman lead Valerie and Roxanne to
the Churchyard. Frightened, Roxanne whispers to Valerie.

                    ROXANNE
          You talked to the wolf.

                    VALERIE
          It talked to us.

                    ROXANNE
          No. It growled.
                    (off Valerie's look)
          You heard it talk to you?

Valerie glances around to see if anyone has overheard.

                    VALERIE
          They'll call me a witch. Don't tell
          anyone.

                    ROXANNE
          Of course not.

The Captain ushers the Girls toward the Church doors.

                    ROXANNE
          I have to find my brother—

                    VALERIE
          And my parents—

                    SOLOMON
          No one leaves until daybreak.

The Captain shoves them inside.

EXT.   CHURCH - DAWN

As the sun's first light hits the Church door, we see it
creak open. Valerie slips out through the fog.

PATRICK SANCHEZ SMITH POSED FOR THE WEREWOLF FOR THE CHURCH DOOR DESIGN.

EXT.   VILLAGE - CHURCH SQUARE - DAWN (SNOW FALLING)

A light snow drifts down, dusting trampled bodies. The
aftermath of the Wolf's massacre.

Under Lance Man's supervision, Henry and the Tavern Owner
help the Undertakers load a frozen body onto the Cart.
It's THE REEVE.

The Captain and Solomon walk past the Undertakers' Cart.
Solomon looks at the carnage, then the Villagers. Father
Auguste steps forward.

                    FATHER AUGUSTE
          We were wrong to have doubted you.
          We're at your service.

                    SOLOMON
          I've never seen a beast as strong as
          this.
                    (thinking it through)
          A creature this powerful must come
          from a long, uninterrupted bloodline.
          Each generation is more potent than
          the one before.

Solomon stares at the bodies of the dead. Appalled.

                    SOLOMON
          I don't just want to kill this animal.
          Not anymore. I want to make it
          suffer. We'll have to find it in its
          human form.

                    CAPTAIN
          How? You said it yourself: It could
          be any of them.

Solomon steps into the crowd, circling the Villagers,
looking into their eyes... Peter, Valerie, Prudence,
Rose, Roxanne, Henry, the Tavern Owner...

                    SOLOMON
          It hasn't survived this long by
          being obvious. Look everywhere. The
          signs will be subtle: Isolation.
          Witchcraft. Black arts. Abnormal
          behavior. Strange smells.
                    (to the Villagers)
          Your homes will be searched. Your
          secrets will be brought to light.

Valerie and the Villagers are suddenly very aware of
the Soldiers around them. And the weapons in their
hands.

                    SOLOMON
          If you are innocent, you have
          nothing to fear. But if you are
          guilty, I swear on my children...
                    (beat)
          ...you will be destroyed.

Suddenly, there is a low MOAN from behind the well. The
Captain rushes over to see his Brother, crumpled to the
ground, his arm slashed. The Captain crouches near him.

these guys had to lie facedown
in the DOLOMITE all day.
DOLOMITE is the white sand
we used for snow - on the ground.
we grew to Love it...

105

CAPTAIN
Bring me water! Hurry!

Valerie rushes over with her bucket. The wound is
discolored, infected. Something horrible is happening.

Solomon's hand goes to his sword. The Captain stands up.

SOLOMON
It's a Blood Moon, so he must...

CAPTAIN
He's my brother.

THE MASKED BOWMAN

Solomon ignores him. <u>He draws his sword and abruptly</u>
<u>plunges it into the Brother's heart.</u> The crowd startles.

                    SOLOMON
        A man bitten is a man cursed.

Stunned silence. The Captain's eyes narrow. Deeply
disturbed, Valerie grabs her pail and rushes off.

ACROSS THE SQUARE, Peter races after Valerie.

                    PETER (O.S.)
        Valerie!

FATHER SOLOMON

INT./EXT.   VALERIE'S FAMILY COTTAGE - DAY

Leaving the chain lock on, Valerie cracks open the door.

                    VALERIE
          Peter...

Valerie looks at Peter's *dark brown eyes*. Is he the wolf?

Panicked, Valerie doesn't open the door, but talks through
the crack. He pushes on the door—it cracks slightly under
the pressure. Behind him, across the street, Bolas Man
and Tizona Man BREAK DOWN the door to a cottage and start
SEARCHING the house.

                         PETER
          Valerie, open the door.

                         VALERIE
                    (she doesn't)
          You shouldn't be here.

                         PETER
          We're all in danger. We've got to go.

He sees the hesitation in her eyes. She sees a hint of
anger in his.

                         PETER
          Get your things. We're leaving now.
          Come away with me.

Her face darkens. Something about what he just said...?

                         VALERIE
          I can't go now. My mother's been hurt.

Peter is devastated. Frustration boiling into anger.

                         VALERIE
          I don't have a choice. I'm sorry.

She hears a LOUD NOISE from inside the house. She SHUTS
the door and BOLTS it.

INSIDE, Valerie turns around and GASPS.

A HUGE, DARK FIGURE CROUCHES OVER HER MOTHER'S INERT BODY.

Valerie staggers backward. Wind whistles through the walls—
the fire shifts.

She now sees: The flickering firelight has distorted the
shadow of her GRANDMOTHER, who is changing Suzette's
bandages. Her shadow shape-shifts on the wall.

Valerie is overwhelmed: *Is her grandmother the Wolf?*

109

Valerie steps into the alcove and stares at Suzette's horrible *claw marks*, then at Grandmother's *fingernails*...

Scared, Valerie surreptitiously slips an ELKHORN KITCHEN KNIFE into her cuff, when—

A HAND GRABS HER.

VALERIE FREEZES IN FEAR.

But it's <u>Suzette.</u> Her poor mother. Valerie exhales.

> SUZETTE
> Don't leave me... alone...

Grandmother helps Suzette drink a cup of the sleeping tea. Valerie watches her carefully.

GRANDMOTHER
Rest, dear...

Valerie and Grandmother tiptoe into the kitchen. They start to wash the bandages in a bucket. Grandmother sees the troubled look on Valerie's face. As they work...

GRANDMOTHER
What is it, darling? Do you want to tell me?

It's not really a question. Valerie looks into Grandmother's eyes. They are *dark brown*. Burning. Almost *compelling* Valerie to answer...

111

                         VALERIE
            The... the Wolf. It talked to me.

Grandmother is startled. Scared.

                         GRANDMOTHER
            And you understood it?

Grandmother stares at Valerie *suspiciously*. *Grandmother*
secretly slips a PAIR OF SCISSORS into her hand.

                         VALERIE
            As clearly as I understand you.

Valerie looks directly into Grandmother's eyes. She almost
shivers. She clenches the hidden knife.

                         GRANDMOTHER
            Who have you told about this?

The tension is thick. Both women look eerie in the
firelight. Every breath is measured.

                         VALERIE
            Only Roxanne knows, but she won't tell
            anyone. She won't even talk to me about
            it.

Grandmother thinks for a beat. Then she steps closer...
GRIPPING THE SCISSORS... testing her...?

                         GRANDMOTHER
            It chose not to kill you...

                         VALERIE
                        (realizing)
            I think... it wants me alive.

Valerie steps away from the fire—she opens the shutters.
In the soft light of the window, she looks so innocent.
Grandmother releases the scissors: *What was she thinking?*
This is her darling granddaughter.

                         GRANDMOTHER
            But why you, Valerie?

Valerie looks at her grandmother in the soft light. She
tucks the knife away: *What was she thinking?* This is her
dear grandmother. Concerned.

                         VALERIE
            I don't know. But if I don't go with
            it, it will kill everyone I love. It's
            already killed Lucie...

112

Grandmother squeezes Valerie's hand.

> VALERIE
> It's coming for me, before the moon
> wanes.

> GRANDMOTHER
> That's only two days from now.

> VALERIE
> I don't know what to do...

Upset, Grandmother wraps an arm around Valerie. Suzette MOANS, and Grandmother rushes to her side. Valerie looks down at the wooden bucket—the bandages have turned the water BLOOD RED. She picks up the pail and heads out for water.

EXT. VILLAGE - VARIOUS - DAY

Valerie leaves her cottage carrying the bucket...

UNKNOWN POV: Someone is watching her. Following her...

She passes Bolas Man and Tizona Man searching cottages. Neighbors peer out windows, too scared to interfere.

UNKNOWN POV: Tracking Valerie as she walks toward the square. We're getting closer to her, closing in...

Just then, Valerie sees Marguerite and Roxanne approaching with full water buckets, on their way home from the well. Valerie pauses to speak to them...

UNKNOWN POV: Her Stalker ducks back out of sight.

> VALERIE
> (to Roxanne)
> Has Claude come home?

But Roxanne brushes past her without answering.

> MARGUERITE
> Nobody's seen him.

Valerie watches them go, unsettled by Roxanne's behavior. As they walk away, Valerie thinks she sees movement...

UNKNOWN POV:... but her Stalker remains hidden, watching. After a beat, Valerie continues on her way. Her Stalker emerges, following her...

113

...TO THE WELL. There's no one else here. Valerie
startles, turns—

It's Henry. Valerie eyes him, wary.

                    Henry
          I saw you with Peter.

FLASH: *arching her back in the Granary.*

Valerie looks away, embarrassed. But Henry steps right up
close—almost touching her. Her breath quickens.

                    Henry
               (his heart breaking)
          I know you don't want me... like
          that...
               (she doesn't contradict him)
          I'm not going to force you to marry
          me.
               (she still says nothing)
          I'll break off the engagement...

Valerie removes Henry's bracelet and hands it to him.

                    VALERIE
          It's lovely.

Emotionally demolished, Henry pockets the bracelet and
walks away.

Valerie heads for home. She passes the Masked Bowman
ransacking a shop.

Solomon and the Captain supervise as Lance Man and Kusa
Man search cottages. Throwing out the family's meager
possessions.

Suddenly, there's a commotion and the Soldiers rush
toward the Granary Tower. Valerie and other Villagers
chase after them.

INT./EXT. GRANARY - WOLF TEMPLE SQUARE - DAY

A crowd pushes its way into the Granary. In the crush of
the mob, Valerie spots ROXANNE. She's sobbing and LOOKING
UP. Valerie follows her look:

Claude has climbed up the hopper shaft to a platform.
Scared, trembling. Below is Father Auguste, standing with
Solomon and his soldiers, weapons at the ready.

ROXANNE launches herself at Solomon, but the Masked
Bowman instantly blocks her.

Andy Cheng suggested giving each soldier a unique weapon and skill set

Valerie pushes through the crowd and stands beside
Roxanne. She looks at Solomon, trying to connect.

> VALERIE
> I saw him at the festival—he's not
> the Wolf. He hasn't done anything!

> SOLOMON
> I want him interrogated. Look at
> him...

He gestures to the roof. THEIR POV: UP ON THE
PLATFORM, Claude looks down at them, crouched like a
GARGOYLE. Scared. Agitated. He does seem possessed.

> SOLOMON
> His speech is twisted—he communes
> with demons.

> VALERIE
> That can't be... I know him!

> SOLOMON
> Better than I knew my own wife?

Valerie doesn't have a quick answer to that. Solomon
shows her a battered tarot card. Valerie stares at his
gleaming silver fingernails.

> SOLOMON
> This was found near the body of
> your dead sister. He practices the
> dark arts.

> MADAME Lazar
> (stepping up)
> *He's a conjurer.* I saw it for the
> Devil's work, but they gave him
> money!

Villagers chime in, supporting her. Valerie stares at
Madame Lazar's beady eyes: They are *deep brown.*

> VALERIE
> Just because he's *different* doesn't
> mean he's guilty.

> MADAME LAZAR
> Innocent people don't run.

                    SOLOMON
                (to the Soldiers)
         Get him down from there.

Kusa Man and Tizona Man turn down their hinged boot
spurs, making them into CLIMBING SPIKES. Using HAND
SCYTHES and the spikes, they start climbing the walls.

Kusa Man and Tizona Man TRAP Claude on the top
platform, brandishing their scythes.

EXT. GRANARY TOWER - WOLF TEMPLE SQUARE - DAY

Valerie watches Lance Man carry Claude away.

                    ROXANNE
              (turning to Father Auguste)
         Can't you do something?

But Father Auguste avoids her gaze. Ashamed.

Valerie spots Peter in the crowd. They make eye
contact—but there is a distance between them now, an
uncertainty.

Then—ROXANNE steps in front of Valerie and picks up
something on the ground, lying in the mud. She shows it
to Valerie: one of Claude's tarot cards—THE FOOL.

EXT. GRANARY BARN - DUSK

Solomon is using the Granary Barn as a makeshift
headquarters. Kusa Man and Lance Man drag Claude to
the BRAZEN ELEPHANT. There's a door in the elephant's
belly. A fire burns beneath it, heating the brass to a
red-hot glow.

                    SOLOMON
         Tell me the name of the Wolf.

Claude stares at him. Silent, confused. Solomon nods—
the Soldiers stuff Claude inside and SLAM the door.

                    SOLOMON
         Tell me the name.

Claude THRASHES inside the hot metal container. He
doesn't say a name; he just screams in pain. Father
Auguste's disillusionment with Solomon is growing.

                    SOLOMON
         The Romans invented this. It's an
         ingenious system for extracting the
         truth.

117

                    FATHER AUGUSTE
          How can he give you a name? The boy
          can barely speak.

Father Solomon listens to the screams. The FLAMES gleam
off the brass Elephant, casting him in hellfire.

                    SOLOMON
          Listen to how he sings of his love of
          Satan...

This is too much for Father Auguste. He recoils—but
Solomon places a firm hand on his shoulder.

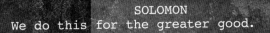

SOLOMON
We do this for the greater good.

FATHER AUGUSTE
What is the good in this?

SOLOMON
I killed my wife to protect my children.
Our methods of pleasing God are sometimes
flawed, but this is the business of werewolf
hunting. You'd best develop a stomach for
it.

The early concept art by Spectral Motion shows that we were originally using the classic Greek BRAZEN BULL. But we found out that another movie was shooting a scene with a BULL—so we switched to an ELEPHANT.

119

INT. TAVERN - LATE NIGHT

A close-up of razor-sharp fingernails plated with silver
ripping through rare pink venison. Track back to reveal that
these bare hands belong to Father Solomon. WHOA.

The Captain ushers Roxanne in past another Soldier guarding
the door.

                              CAPTAIN
            She says it's important.

120

Solomon stares as she nervously steps forward and drops some meager COINS on the table.

                    ROXANNE
          I'd like to bargain for the release of my
          brother.

Solomon laughs at the meager coins.

                    CAPTAIN
          Get out.

But Roxanne stands frozen, gathering her courage.

                    ROXANNE
          I have more than money to offer.

Trembling, she opens her cloak, showing Solomon her bodice and bare shoulders. Solomon eyes her.

                    SOLOMON
          Turn around.

Roxanne chokes back tears and does as instructed.

                    SOLOMON
          Is this your idea of a bribe?

The Captain laughs. Roxanne covers herself, humiliated. Solomon nods and the Captain drags her away, struggling.

                    ROXANNE
          Wait. I have something else.

Solomon looks at her: Roxanne hesitates. This is the worst moment of her life. So far.

                    ROXANNE
          Spare my brother, and I'll tell you the
          name of a witch.

                    SOLOMON
          Now, *that* is worth something.

INT. TAVERN - DAY

The bar is arranged like a makeshift courtroom. Everyone's here: bleary-eyed Cesaire, Grandmother, and Suzette in a scarf. Peter in the back.

Valerie stands in front, wearing shackles. Solomon and Roxanne stand next to her. Roxanne can't look at Valerie.

SOLOMON
Tell them what you told me.

ROXANNE
She can climb the tallest trees. She can
run faster than all the girls...

CESAIRE
I taught her to climb—

Tizona Man, guarding the family, unsheathes his sword and
extends it toward Cesaire. Solomon prods Roxanne to continue.

ROXANNE
...She wears a red cloak. The Devil's color.

GRANDMOTHER
I made her that cloak—

Now, Kusa Man pulls out his dagger and threatens her.
Suzette pulls her back. Solomon stares at Roxanne.

ROXANNE
(reluctant)
And she can talk to werewolves. I've
seen it with my own eyes.

Low MURMURS. Shock. Surprise. Solomon turns to Valerie.

SOLOMON
Do you deny it?

Valerie takes a deep breath.

VALERIE
No. I don't deny it.

The crowd REACTS. Solomon quiets them with a look.

SOLOMON
And what was the nature of this
conversation?

                    VALERIE
          No disrespect, but it said you don't
          know what you're dealing with.

Solomon bristles. Barely concealing his fury.

                    SOLOMON
          Indeed. What else did it say?

                    VALERIE
          It promised to leave Daggörhorn in
          peace. But only if I leave with it.

Roxanne is stunned. Peter reacts. A heavy silence falls
over the room. Solomon leans in close to Valerie.

                    SOLOMON
                  (whispering)
          The Wolf is someone in this village
          who wants you, Valerie.
                  (leans in even closer)
          Do you know who it is? I'd think very
          hard if I were you. Tell me. Give me a
          name.

Valerie is terrified, but she will not name anyone. Done
with her, Solomon turns to the Villagers.

                    SOLOMON (CONT'D)
          It wants her, not you. If you want to
          save yourselves... simply give it what
          it wants.

Henry is horrified. On his feet in an instant, outraged.

                    HENRY
          We can't give her to the Wolf. That's
          human sacrifice.

Madame Lazar, still in her mourning dress, turns to him.

                    MADAME LAZAR
          We've all made sacrifices.

Henry looks around for support. The Villagers avert their
eyes, too afraid of being accused themselves. Solomon nods
for Lance Man to take Valerie out.

Father Auguste approaches Solomon.

> FATHER AUGUSTE
> I thought you came to kill the Wolf,
> not appease it.

> SOLOMON
> I have no intention of appeasing it.

EXT. TAVERN - CHURCH SQUARE - DAY

CAMERA FINDS Cesaire, Suzette, and Grandmother leaving
the Tavern side door. They overhear MADAME LAZAR, eyes
burning as she talks to Rose and some GOSSIPMONGERS on
the street below.

> MADAME LAZAR
> Her grandmother lives all alone in
> the woods. The first victim was her
> sister. The second was her fiancé's
> father. And don't forget her poor
> mother, scarred for life. If the
> girl isn't a witch, then how do you
> explain it?

Walking past the Gossipmongers, GRANDMOTHER actually
seems to be paying attention. Upset, Cesaire notices.

THE TAVERN

126

                   GRANDMOTHER
    No. Lucie wouldn't do that, but she
    might have responded to Henry.

Lance Man approaches—the visit is over. Grandmother exits,
thinking... The pieces are fitting together. She hands the
food and blanket to Lance Man.

                   GRANDMOTHER
    Make sure she gets this.

Lance Man nods, opens the parcel, and takes a bite of the
apple. Grandmother slaps it out of his hand. Another Guard
grabs her from behind and drags her away.

INT. BLACKSMITH'S SHOP - DAY

Henry is hammering out <u>a key of some kind.</u> There is a
knock on the door. Henry answers without looking up.

                    HENRY
          We're closed.

Grandmother enters, sets down a parcel, and gives Henry
a friendly hug.

                    GRANDMOTHER
          Hello, Henry. I brought you some
          cookies. I just wanted to thank you
          for speaking up this morning. That
          was very brave.

                    HENRY
          I said what I felt.

                    GRANDMOTHER
          You're under no obligation to stand
          in Valerie's defense. You broke off
          your engagement to her.

                    HENRY
          She's in love with someone else.
          That doesn't mean I stopped caring
          about her.

Henry dips the strange-looking key he's working on into
a tub of water. HIIISSS...

                    GRANDMOTHER
          I imagine that's just the same way
          Lucie felt about you.

Henry looks up: What's this about? He shrugs it off.

                    HENRY
          She had a crush on me.

                    GRANDMOTHER
          Valerie just told me. Lucie probably
          would have done anything for you.
          She would have even agreed to meet
          you on a Wolf Night, if you asked
          her to.

Henry is bewildered, angry. STEAM rises from the tub.

                    HENRY
          Why are you doing this? Do you
          think I'm the Wolf? Are you
          accusing me of murder?

                    GRANDMOTHER
          I'm not accusing anyone of
          anything. I'm trying to find out
          the truth.

As she says this, a slow look of dawning realization comes over him. Realization and horror.

                    HENRY
          It's you. My God, it's you. I can
          smell it on you now.

                    GRANDMOTHER
          What can you smell on me?

Nervous, Grandmother inches even closer to the door.

                    HENRY
          The night my father died. I could
          smell the Wolf. A deep musk.
                    (he steps closer)
          And I smell it on you right now.

Upset, Grandmother inhales. Maybe realizing something? But now Henry stands too close to her.

                    HENRY (CONT'D)
          What were you doing out there in
          that cabin all by yourself? On the
          night Lucie died?

Grandmother's trying to process this...

                    GRANDMOTHER
          Henry, I read until I fell asleep.

                    HENRY
          And then what? You don't know, do
          you?

                    GRANDMOTHER
          Don't try to turn this on me... I
          know what you're doing.

Grandmother turns and walks out the door—

EXT. BLACKSMITH'S SHOP - DAY

—and almost collides with Peter, who's chopping firewood into KINDLING, when—

A strange coughing sound disturbs Grandmother. She looks up. Madame Lazar stares at her from the second-floor window. Spooked, Grandmother turns and heads down the path to the woods. Madame Lazar watches her go...

INT. GRANDMOTHER'S COTTAGE - DAY

Grandmother opens the silk curtain that conceals her
bedchamber. At the foot of her bed is her ornate HOPE
CHEST. She kneels. After a long beat, she opens it.

EXT. VILLAGE - WOLF TEMPLE SQUARE - LATE AFTERNOON

Few Villagers are out. PETER stacks KINDLING near the
BUTCHER SHOP. He nods to—

CESAIRE, who pushes the kerosene barrel around the Square
in a wheelbarrow. Taking nips from his flask. He exchanges
a conspiratorial look with Peter.

No one else notices that the barrel is leaking. Cesaire is
nonchalantly leaving a trail of kerosene in the snow.

Suddenly, the Captain steps up, flanked by Kusa Man. Cesaire
stands between the barrel of kerosene and the Captain, trying
to hide it. What do they know?

                    CAPTAIN
          You're coming with us.

Cesaire panics. He makes a run for it, drawing the Soldiers
away from the barrel, CHARGING through the snow, LEAPING over
a horse trough. The Captain cracks his whip around Cesaire's
ankle, tripping him up.

Cesaire face-plants in a snowdrift, and the Soldiers are on
him in an instant, wrenching his arms behind his back and
dragging him to his feet. He struggles.

                    CESAIRE
          I haven't done anything—

                    CAPTAIN
          Just a precaution. Father Solomon doesn't
          want any trouble from the witch's family.

The Captain and Kusa Man haul him away.

INT. GRANARY BARN - LATE AFTERNOON

Solomon approaches Valerie's cell. He opens the gate and
holds out her cloak to her.

                    SOLOMON
          Put on your harlot's robe.

Valerie reluctantly slips into the Red Riding Hood. Its beauty
seems strange in this awful place.

Lance Man, the guard, replaces the iron manacles on her
wrists. Valerie is frightened as she walks to her death.

Just then, the Captain and Kusa Man haul Cesaire inside
and drag him toward the cell. Cesaire is bruised, badly
beaten. Cesaire looks at his terrified daughter, going to
her death. He searches for words...

                    CESAIRE
          I tried to protect you. You and Lucie...

                    VALERIE
          It's all right, Papa... You taught us
          to be strong.

                    CESAIRE
          Yes. Now, stay strong, Valerie.

The Captain slams Cesaire roughly into the cell.

EXT. GRANARY BARN - LATE AFTERNOON

Lance Man leads Valerie outside. The Captain approaches
with a HUMILIATION MASK: an iron mask with tiny eyeholes.
This one is shaped like a Wolf. The Villagers line the
street, fascinated by the surreal image.

EXT. VILLAGE - CHURCH SQUARE - LATE AFTERNOON

Solomon and his Soldiers ride their horses in a macabre
parade down the street. Valerie, chained to Lance Man,
trudges behind them in the IRON WOLF MASK.

Solomon and Father Auguste step up to the Wolf Temple.
Valerie is placed on the altar with the mask still on.

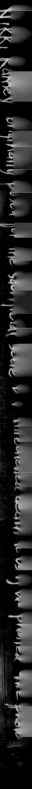

EXT. VILLAGE - WOLF TEMPLE SQUARE - LATE AFTERNOON

As the Villagers watch, Valerie is placed on the altar
with the mask still on. The Captain snaps TWO LOCKS into
place.

Father Auguste blesses her, then he and Solomon walk away
across the square as...

VALERIE'S POV THROUGH THE MASK: SUZETTE suddenly marches
up to Solomon.

                    SUZETTE
          Let her go, you bastard.

She raises her hand to slap him. But he CATCHES HER
WRIST.

                    SOLOMON
          You should go home. You should all go
          home.

Through the holes in her mask, Valerie watches as the
Villagers lead her struggling mother away.

EXT. VILLAGE - WOLF TEMPLE SQUARE - CONTINUOUS

Valerie slumps on the altar.

VALERIE'S POV THROUGH THE MASK: Everyone leaves.
They disappear into their homes, bolting their doors.
Suddenly...

A DARK FIGURE BLOCKS THE EYEHOLES OF THE MASK.

Valerie GASPS. Steels herself. THIS IS IT.

Then PRUDENCE leans into her view. Valerie exhales.

                    PRUDENCE
          Valerie? Roxanne wanted you to know
          how sorry she is. She only said those
          things to save her brother.

                    VALERIE
          I know. Will you tell her that I
          forgive her?

                    PRUDENCE
          Of course. But, I wanted to say... I
          don't know what to say.

                    VALERIE
          You don't have to say anything.

140

                    PRUDENCE
          I want to. I want you to know that
          you may have fooled Roxanne, but
          you don't fool me. Not anymore. You
          were always too good. Too pretty.
          Too perfect. You tricked us. And now
          you're going to get what you deserve.

                    VALERIE
          Prudence, I think you'd better go.

Prudence looks up. The sun has almost set.

                    PRUDENCE
          Yes. It won't be long now. The Wolf is
          coming.

UNKNOWN POV - HIGH ANGLE: Prudence walks away from the
altar. Valerie is left alone.

INT. GRANARY TOWER - ACROSS WOLF TEMPLE SQUARE - DUSK

The UNKNOWN POV is from the top platform of the Granary.
IT'S SOLOMON. From here, he has perfect view of the Wolf
Temple. He stares at Valerie: The Wolf Head Mask on her
perfect body.

Father Auguste climbs up a Spiral Stair and sees that the
top platform of the Granary has been converted into a
temporary command center: trunks full of weapons, ropes,
quivers. The Masked Bowman, the Captain, and Kusa Man
sharpen silver-tipped arrows.

Solomon grins and addresses Father Auguste.

                    SOLOMON
          Do you know how you kill a tiger,
          Father Auguste? You tie out your best
          goat and wait.

EXT. VILLAGE - WOLF TEMPLE SQUARE - NIGHT

A wicked winter wind HOWLS. The crimson moon is huge,
casting the night in blood. It's an evil night.

Valerie waits on the altar, nerves frayed. Tizona Man and
Bolas Man hide in two high SNIPER POSITIONS across the
square. Lance Man is tucked into an alley. The Soldiers
watch in tense silence, ready with silver-tipped arrows.
Atop the Granary, Solomon gazes out at the darkness.
Obsessed. Like Captain Ahab scanning the high seas for
his white whale.

But unseen by everyone, a DARK FIGURE crouches by a crumbled wall. The Figure lowers a torch, touching it to the line of kerosene that Cesaire left in the snow and...

FWOOF! *The FLAMES illuminate the Figure. It's PETER.*

IN THE GRANARY, *all eyes turn to the* FLAMES as a ring of fire leaps up. The FIRE tracks the kerosene trail all the way around to the BUTCHER SHOP... and the kindling we saw Peter stacking earlier. Suddenly, the shop is in FLAMES.

IN THE GRANARY - TOP PLATFORM. Solomon signals Tizona, Bolas, and Kusa. They rappel down from their sniper positions and join Lance Man to fight the fire.

VALERIE'S POV THROUGH THE MASK: She watches the Soldiers kick snow on the flames. Suddenly—

—a Cloaked Man whispers in her ear. It's Henry.

                    HENRY
          I'm going to get you out of here.

Henry pulls out a ring with the STRANGE-LOOKING KEYS we saw him making earlier. They're skeleton keys. He sets about picking the locks. He opens the first one quickly.

AT THE BUTCHER SHOP, the Soldiers battle the fire. Smoke billows out, obscuring the altar.

PETER sneaks into the GRANARY and starts to light the hay, when—

WHACK! The blade of the Kusarigama KNOCKS the torch out of his hand. WHAM! Kusa Man SNARES his leg with the KUSARIGAMA CHAIN. They wrestle as the FLAMES catch the Granary walls...

IN THE GRANARY—TOP PLATFORM—Solomon starts the evacuation. He heads down the Spiral Stair first, of course—followed by the Masked Bowman and Father Auguste. ON THE MIDDLE PLATFORM, Solomon sees the Cloaked Man (Henry) through the window. He yells to the Masked Bowman.

                    SOLOMON
          He's taken the bait.

ON THE BRIDGE, the Masked Bowman aims his crossbow.

ON THE MIDDLE PLATFORM, Father Auguste looks out the window and squints through the smoke. HIS POV: The shape is clearly a MAN, not a BEAST.

                    FATHER AUGUSTE
          Wait—it's not the Wolf.

                    SOLOMON
          He's aiding a witch.
                    (to the Masked Bowman)
          Shoot!!

ON THE BRIDGE, the Masked Bowman takes aim—but Father Auguste charges him, spoiling the shot. The arrow WHIZZES by Henry's head. Father Auguste calls out:

                    FATHER AUGUSTE
          RUN!

Solomon rushes to Father Auguste and plunges a dagger into Father Auguste's back. Then Father Auguste crumples. The lifeless body of the holy man PLUMMETS OFF THE BRIDGE.

Solomon watches as Valerie and the Cloaked Man escape.

ON THE MIDDLE PLATFORM, Solomon steps inside and heads down the stairs, disturbed by what he's done. The Masked Bowman and the Captain follow.

OUTSIDE THE GRANARY, Lance Man and Kusa Man approach Solomon with Peter in manacles.

                    LANCE MAN
          This one started the fire.

Solomon looks at Peter—eyes narrowing.

                    SOLOMON
          Lock him up. In the elephant.

INT. RUINS - THE BRAZEN ELEPHANT - NIGHT

Lance Man opens the door to the Brazen Elephant, and Kusa Man SHOVES Peter inside. Then the door is SLAMMED shut and LOCKED. The Soldiers race back to the Square.

EXT. RECTORY ALLEY - NIGHT

Henry has led Valerie away, running, She looks back. She hears Soldiers giving chase.

                              Henry
                Come on... Peter's meeting us with
                horses at the vats...

EXT.   VILLAGE - NEAR WOLF TEMPLE SQUARE - NIGHT

Solomon and the Captain are raising the alarm.

                              SOLOMON
                The witch has escaped!

INT.   RUINS - NIGHT

The Brazen Elephant is rocking. Back and forth. We hear
the SOUNDS of tremendous violence from inside. A body
banging against metal, muffled sounds. The statue sways
on its platform...

                              PETER (O.S.)
                ...Valerie...

Peter's voice is twisted into something inhuman... like
the VOICE OF A BEAST.

EXT.   DYE SHOP - NIGHT

Henry leads Valerie around the back of the Dye Shop and
stops short. Shimmering vats of blue dye and towers of
blue petals, but nothing else. No Peter. No horses.

                              VALERIE
                Where's Peter?

                              HENRY
                I don't know. He should be here by
                now.

Valerie looks around: She is alone with Henry in a dark,
secluded place. Clouds drift across the Blood Moon.

                              HENRY
                If he doesn't show, I'll take you
                away...

Valerie's suspicion grows. She takes a step back from him
and raises the knife, ready to strike, but hears... the
faraway GROWL of the Wolf. The strange mix of human and
animal sounds, male and female...

Valerie looks at Henry, realizing what that means. In
shock, she looks at the knife in her hand. Then Henry
turns and sees the knife as well.

                    VALERIE
          Oh, my God. I'm so sorry, Henry...
          You're not the Wolf.

                    Henry
               (easing the tension)
          Right. Now, could you put that blade
          away?

She sheepishly returns the blade to her boot, when—
another GROWL. Valerie has an awful thought...

                    VALERIE
          Henry, when was the last time you saw
          Peter?

But Henry does not answer, because he spots Bolas Man and
Tizona Man looking for them in the Rectory Alley. He and
Valerie duck into a Wool-Storage Area. Pressed up against
the back wall, in the shadows. The Soldiers draw closer.

Valerie and Henry HEAR... in the distance, other Soldiers
searching the village. Henry whispers to Valerie...

                    Henry
          ...We're trapped...

                    VALERIE
          The church. Even Solomon can't violate
          the protection of sanctuary. And the
          Wolf can't cross onto holy ground.

Now Henry looks at her, full of yearning, and puts his
hand on her waist. Valerie stops breathing as he slides
his hand down her leg and...

PULLS THE KNIFE FROM HER BOOT. Valerie breathes again.

Henry STABS THE KNIFE between two boards in the wall
behind them. He pries a board loose, then kicks it down.

EXT.   VILLAGE - WOOL-STORAGE AREA - NIGHT

Valerie and Henry RUN for it. She hears the SOLDIERS
searching the town, the shouts of Villagers. But even
with all this... Valerie hears...

THE WOLF WHISPER HER NAME. But from where? She looks to
Henry, running beside her. He hasn't heard. Now she looks
out the Main Gate and sees A DARK SHAPE running through
the trees.

                    WOLF (IN VALERIE'S HEAD)
          ...Valerie...

Valerie looks back and sees Tizona Man and Bolas Man
behind them, searching the Dye Shop Alley. They turn the
corner... into...

EXT. DYE SHOP ALLEY - WOOL-STORAGE AREA - NIGHT

Bolas Man and Tizona Man STORM the Wool-Storage Area.
They CLOSE IN on the back wall where Valerie and Henry
just were... BUT THEY'RE GONE.

EXT. CHURCH SQUARE - NIGHT

There it is... the Church. Valerie and Henry RUN FOR IT...
out into the square. Valerie hears the LOW GROWL behind
her... Henry pulls her on.

halfway across the square now. Closer to the Church. But
from a balcony, the Masked Bowman raises his crossbow AND
FIRES...

The arrow flies hot, straight, and true, right for Valerie,
but it does not hit her because... Henry DIVES IN FRONT
and TAKES THE ARROW instead.

It PUNCHES him in the left shoulder and DIGS DEEP into his
body. Henry tries to be stoic to ward off the pain.

                    HENRY
          Go, Valerie. GO.

But she will not leave him. She looks into his eyes:
This guy is amazing. She throws his good arm around her
shoulder, and together they run the last 25 yards for
sanctuary.

A STONE GATE marks the entrance to the Holy Ground... But
Solomon blocks their way. The Captain beside him.

                    VALERIE
          We claim sanctuary.

                    SOLOMON
          You're not on holy ground yet.

Solomon grips the arrow in Henry's shoulder.

                    SOLOMON
                (he pulls out arrow)
          And this belongs to me.

Henry grits his teeth against the pain. The Captain YANKS
him inside the Church wall.

Then Valerie hears it again, that voice in her head...

> The WOLF (IN VALERIE'S HEAD)
> ...Valerie...

Now she turns and there it is. By the Tavern.

The WOLF. Staring at Valerie with glowing eyes. Tizona Man
and Bolas Man are dead on the ground behind it. The Main
Gate is open. Valerie is paralyzed with fear as the Wolf
CHARGES directly at her.

Solomon looks at the eastern horizon—it's starting to glow.
He whispers to the Captain.

> SOLOMON
> We can stall. It's almost daybreak.

Solomon GRABS Valerie's hair—JERKS her back—puts his sword
to her neck and uses Valerie as a HUMAN SHIELD. Solomon
calls out to the Wolf...

> SOLOMON
> You want her alive, don't you?

The Wolf glares at Solomon, then looks urgently to the
east. The sky is getting lighter. Kusa Man and Lance Man
race out of the alley and into the Churchyard.

Henry RUSHES toward Valerie, but Lance Man holds him
back. The Masked Bowman is now positioned on a nearby
roof, crossbow at the ready.

                    SOLOMON
               (to the Masked Bowman)
          Kill it!

The Masked Bowman PULLS the trigger—the Wolf JUMPS—
the bolt MISSES and SMASHES a window. Solomon releases
Valerie and brandishes his sword. Fearless, full of
bloodlust, SOLOMON CHARGES THE WOLF, THRUSTING his sword.

But the Wolf DODGES his blows, LUNGES, and CLAMPS down
on Solomon's wrist—CRUNCHES THROUGH BONE, biting off his
hand. Solomon lets loose a blood-curdling scream.

The HAND falls into the snow, silver fingernails
clutching the silver sword. Useless now.

The Captain CRACKS his WHIP at the Wolf but misses,
and the Wolf CHARGES him and SNATCHES his SHIELD, then
FLINGS it. It SLAMS into the Masked Bowman.

Curious Villagers, including Roxanne, approach from
behind the Church, careful to stay on SACRED GROUND.

                    THE WOLF
         Valerie, you can't hide from this.

The Wolf WHIRLS around and STOPS just before the Gate.
The Wolf and Valerie stare at each other. Transfixed.

The Wolf glances at the glowing horizon. Anxious, it
reaches toward Valerie. AS IT CROSSES THE THRESHOLD OF
THE GATE, its PAW STARTS TO CATCH FIRE.

The Wolf retracts—its paw SINGED. The Wolf SNAPS—glaring
at Valerie with all four eyes.

                    THE WOLF
         Step across the gate, or I'll kill
         everyone. Do you understand?

                    VALERIE
         Yes, I understand you.

                    SOLOMON
         See how the Witch talks to the Wolf!

Valerie ignores him and glances at the Villagers.

                    THE WOLF
         Make your decision.

Valerie can't let these people die. She looks back at the
Wolf. And makes an impossible decision.

> VALERIE
> I won't let you destroy my home. I'll
> go with you... to save them.

Valerie takes a step toward the Gate. Roxanne and the
Villagers watch, moved and ashamed by her bravery.

Valerie takes another step. The Wolf awaits, dark and
terrifying. Impatient. There's a glow on the horizon—the
sun is almost up.

Henry LUNGES forward, but Lance Man holds him back.
Heart bursting, Roxanne boldly STEPS in front of Valerie,
careful to remain on Sacred Ground.

> ROXANNE
> I won't let you sacrifice yourself
> for us.

ROSE PUSHES through the crowd and stands next to
Roxanne—facing the Wolf.

                    ROSE
          Nor will I.

MARGUERITE steps up beside her daughter. Other Villagers
join them—forming a human wall.

                  MARGUERITE
          Nor will I.

Finally, even Prudence joins the other Villagers.

                  PRUDENCE
          Nor will I.

All standing on Sacred Ground. All protecting Valerie.

Valerie looks around—the people that turned against her
are now protecting her.

ROSE

ROXANNE

PRUDENCE

154

Then: A ROOSTER CROWS somewhere in the village. The Wolf looks up—the sun is nearly up. If the Wolf doesn't leave now, he will be revealed in his human form.

The WOLF lets loose an UNEARTHLY GROWL. So close to his prize, but unable to cross the Gate and claim it. Furious, the Wolf CHARGES off into the fading night. Everyone is thrilled.

The Villagers relax, triumphant. Valerie hugs Roxanne. Then Solomon rips Valerie away with his good hand and...

> SOLOMON
> You will still burn, witch.

HE SLAMS HER HEAD against a gravestone with a sickening THUD. Henry tries to break away from Lance Man to help Valerie, but Solomon whirls toward him, ready to slash with his sharpened nails, when—

—WHACK! The Captain KICKS Solomon to the ground. He holds Solomon's silver sword in his hand.

> CAPTAIN
> (softly to Solomon)
> Under the Blood Moon. A man bitten is
> a man cursed.

Solomon knows what must be.

> SOLOMON
> My children will be orphans.

> CAPTAIN
> My brother had children, too.

The Captain's words sink in. Solomon nods—realizing what he's become: no better than the beast he hunted.

> SOLOMON
> Forgive your lost sheep, Father. I
> meant only to serve you... to protect
> us from darkness...

The Captain plunges the sword into Solomon's heart. The same way Solomon killed his Brother. And just like Solomon did, he turns to the crowd and says...

Costume Department, under designer Cindy Evans and assistant designer Nancy Bryant, made beautiful color palettes for all the characters and dyed fabrics to match.

155

                         CAPTAIN
           Under the Blood Moon, a man bitten is
           a man cursed.

Suddenly, blood starts trickling out of Valerie's hair
from where she hit the wall. She puts a hand to her head,
feels the blood. She falls to her knees, dizzy.

                         VALERIE
           Where's Peter...?

Then her world blurs—

INT. GRANDMOTHER'S HOUSE - MORNING (SNOW FALLING)

Valerie wakes up... She opens her eyes—everything is
still blurry, but she gradually focuses. Her POV: She's in
her grandmother's bed. Someone is sleeping next to her.
She turns her head slowly and sees...

It's Grandmother, propped up on the pillows, staring
intensely into her eyes.

                         VALERIE
           What big eyes you have, Grandmother.

                         GRANDMOTHER
           The better to see you with, my dear.

Valerie rubs her bruised head—and sees the strange shape
of her Grandmother's ears.

                         VALERIE
           What big ears you have, Grandmother.

                         GRANDMOTHER
           The better to hear you with, my dear.

A chill runs down Valerie's spine as
her grandmother slowly opens her
mouth to smile. Her teeth
look strange.

                         VALERIE
           What big teeth you
           have, Grandmother.

                         GRANDMOTHER
           The better to eat you with,
           my dear.

AND GRANDMOTHER LUNGES AT VALERIE.

Valerie SCREAMS—

INT. VALERIE'S FAMILY COTTAGE - VARIOUS - LATE MORNING

—and then Valerie SNAPS AWAKE in her own bed this time.
The room is IN FOCUS. She tries to shake away the bad
dream, but she is disturbed. Then she cringes painfully.
There's a blood-stained cloth on her head.

156

Roxanne sleeps beside her. She's been here for hours. Valerie grabs her red cloak and climbs down the ladder when she sees her mother SUZETTE, back to the fire, cooking porridge. The fire twists her shadow strangely.

> SUZETTE
> Valerie! You shouldn't be out of bed...
> I was so worried...
>> (gently checking her head wound)
> Oh, it looks better...

Suzette steps to the fire and ladles out a steaming bowl of porridge with raisins. She offers it to Valerie.

> SUZETTE
> I made your favorite, dear.

Valerie notices that her mother's eyes are *dark brown.*

> VALERIE
> Mother, where were you last night?

> SUZETTE
> You saw the neighbors dragging me away.
> I wanted to stay, but... Now, eat up.
> You need your strength.

Valerie stares at the porridge. Uneasy, she steps away. She grabs a wicker basket, opens the door, and steps out.

> SUZETTE
> Where are you going?

> VALERIE
> To Grandmother's.

EXT.   GRANARY BARN - LATE MORNING

The Brazen Elephant now has the door broken open. Its inside is empty. No sign of Peter.

EXT.   VILLAGE - CHURCH SQUARE - LATE MORNING (FLURRIES)

A winter storm is BLOWING in. Valerie kneels in the snow, facing the Church near where Solomon fell. The snow here is still dark with spilled blood.

A MAN CURSED

Bill terezakis of w.c.t. made the severed hand & the wolf head.

157

Then she does something *strange*—she seems to be smoothing the snow... Then she crosses herself. With a look of determination, she grabs the basket, stands, and hurries down the street.

She turns and sees Henry with Kusa Man, Lance Man, and a couple of Villagers gearing up with weapons, saddling up the remaining horses. Henry is wearing pieces of armor.

> HENRY
> We're going after the Wolf before the
> storm can cover its trail. It'll be
> human again. We can finally kill it.
> And I...

Henry hesitates, reluctant to continue. Valerie sees that something is bothering him.

> VALERIE
> What is it? Tell me.

> HENRY
> Peter is still missing... And I'll do
> what I have to do.

Valerie understands all that this means. The Men begin to move out. Henry starts to go, when Valerie takes his good arm, stopping him. Her touch electrifies him.

> VALERIE
> Thank you. For everything.

She stands on her tiptoes and kisses him gently. On the neck... Henry closes his eyes and takes this in.

> Henry
> That's a good start...

He flashes a great smile, then turns and goes with the Men to kill the Wolf.

The Men ride out, tilt up to find Madame Lazar, watching from her second-floor window.

EXT. DARK FOREST - PATH - DAY (SNOWING)

Valerie walks through the snow in her Red Riding Hood, carrying her basket. A HOWLING wind is picking up. Snow swirls through the air around her, drifting across the path and sticking to the trees, giving the forest an eerie, dreamlike feeling.

She hears a branch snap behind her. She WHIRLS around and sees a DARK BLUR through the trees. She runs faster.

It's not fast enough. She hears the footsteps catch up with her. She whips around...

IT'S PETER.

His face is bruised—there's a cut over one eye. And soldier's gloves on his hands. Relief floods over him when he sees Valerie... but she is guarded. He reaches out, but Valerie stiffens. She stares at his gloves.

FLASH: *The Wolf's paw crosses the gate. It burns.*

                    PETER
          Thank God you're all right.

He sees the flicker of fear in her eyes.

                    VALERIE
          Where were you?

                    PETER
               (frustrated, angry)
          I was trapped in that brazen beast all
          night.

Valerie stares at him—searching his dark brown eyes. Looking at his bruises. Peter sees that she's afraid.

                    PETER
          Valerie—what?! You don't believe me?

She doesn't. She takes a frightened step back. Peter steps toward her.

                    VALERIE
          Don't come near me.

Peter steps toward her. Valerie BRANDISHES THE KNIFE.

                    VALERIE
          I'll hurt you, Peter.

                    PETER
          No, you won't.

He takes a quick stride toward her, she SLASHES out with the KNIFE, TEARING through his shirt and RIPPING into Peter's side. His eyes go wide in shock as he sinks to his knees, bleeding in the snow.

Valerie runs through the twisted trees—she's feeling both horror and heartbreak. She has to stop. She looks back.

<u>He's gone.</u> She turns and forces herself to keep running, deeper into the dark woods, toward her grandmother's.

EXT. GRANDMOTHER'S COTTAGE - AFTERNOON (SNOWING HARD)

Valerie POUNDS on the door—pale and quivering, covered in snow.

INT. GRANDMOTHER'S COTTAGE - AFTERNOON (SNOWING OUTSIDE)

Valerie rushes inside, slams the door, and throws the bolt. She looks around: A pot of stew cooks on the fire.

> VALERIE
> Grandmother. Are you all right? I had a
> nightmare—

Did a BLACK SHAPE just dart into the bedchamber?

Valerie nearly JUMPS OUT OF HER SKIN.

Suddenly a MATCH STRIKES—a CANDLE FLARES.

> GRANDMOTHER
> I was dreaming. I'll be out in a minute.
> There's some soup if you're hungry.

VALERIE'S POV THROUGH THE SILK CURTAIN: There is no Wolf. It's just Grandmother, sitting up in bed in her nightie.

Valerie rubs her head wound, gets a hold of herself. She sets down her basket, shivering.

> VALERIE
> I—I think the Wolf is out there.

> GRANDMOTHER
> It's all right, darling. We're safe in
> here. Now, eat up. Remember: All sorrows
> are—

> VALERIE
> —less with bread.

Valerie ladles some stew into a bowl.

> GRANDMOTHER
> That's right. Eat up, my dear.

Valerie takes a bite of the hot stew, then pauses. Dizzy...

> VALERIE
> What is this...?

And Grandmother *stands up.* <u>Pulls off her nightgown</u>, walks toward her, and parts the curtain to reveal...

<u>IT'S CESAIRE.</u> Valerie stands.

> VALERIE
>
> Father? What are you doing here? Where's Grandmother?

> Cesaire
>
> I'm so sorry... she's... dead. I had no choice—she finally realized... what I am.

> VALERIE
>
> What? This can't be... Papa, no. You're joking...

> CESAIRE
>
> I wish I was...

Cesaire picks up Grandmother's nightgown and starts to fold it carefully. Valerie sees that his HAND IS BURNT. <u>From where the Wolf reached across onto holy ground.</u>

> VALERIE
>
> Father. No... How... could you? How could you do this?

> CESAIRE
>
> Oh, Valerie. I wanted you to have a normal childhood—so I've been living a double life. Hiding in plain sight. Living modestly. I tried to keep it up, but I've been so disrespected. Even by my own wife... I've settled for far less than I deserved, and I just couldn't do it anymore. I decided to leave... go to the city... For richer hunting grounds.

> VALERIE
>
> Then why didn't you just go?

165

GRANDMOTHER'S HOUSE

Lead by production designer Tom Sanders and art director Don Macaulay, contsruction coordinaor Charles Leitrants' team built the treehouse, Brent Gloeckler's team sculpted huge trees, and and Jason Claridge's crew painted details and textures to make the house look fairy-tale-old.

CESAIRE
Because I loved you girls, and I
wanted you to come with me. To share
the wealth... A wolf from my own
bloodline would be even more powerful
than I am.

Valerie is putting the pieces together...

VALERIE
But you had to wait 'til the Blood
Moon.

CESAIRE
Yes. By birthright, the gift went
first to my eldest daughter. I know
Lucie loved Henry, so I forged a
letter...

FLASH: *Lucie opens a LETTER: "Meet me in the haystacks
tonight... Henry." Her heart flutters.*

FLASH: *She stands in the field waiting for Henry, but the
Wolf steps up.*

THE WOLF/CESAIRE (V.O.)
*Henry's not coming, Lucie... He's
already asked for your sister's hand in
marriage... But I can give you something
better. Your true power...* But she didn't
understand me. Any offspring of mine
with my wolf blood would have the power
to understand me. Suddenly, it all made
sense. I couldn't be her father... Your
mother lied to me.

FLASH: *The Wolf EXPLODES WITH RAGE and POUNCES on Lucie.*

CESAIRE (V.O.)
Valerie. After all those years of
being so careful, so clever, I lost
control.

VALERIE (V.O.)
Oh, God, so you took revenge on
Mother...

FLASH: *In Cesaire's home, the Wolf mauls Suzette's face.*

CESAIRE
...and her lover.

168

FLASH: *The wolf hunt in the cave. Adrien explores, Henry stops short. This time we see why: Henry freezes behind a rock as the Wolf viciously attacks his father.*

> CESAIRE (V.O.)
> Henry smelled the werewolf that night.
> Then again yesterday...

FLASH: *Grandmother confronts Henry. Grandmother leaves. This time, we see that <u>Cesaire</u> was outside the Blacksmith Shop, helping Peter chop wood. Grandmother inhales...*

> CESAIRE (V.O.) (CONT'D)
> He thought the smell was from your
> grandmother. But she figured it out.
> She's lived with that smell her whole
> life.

FLASH: *Grandmother opens the HOPE CHEST. Now we see: It's filled with men's clothing. Worn and frayed. Grandmother picks up a vest, smells it...*

> CESAIRE (V.O.) (CONT'D)
> You see, my father was a Wolf, too.
> His smell was still on his clothing.
> Your grandmother never knew what it
> meant until... the moment before she
> died.

FLASH: *Grandmother is so distracted that she doesn't notice Cesaire creeping toward her. Full of menace.*

FLASH: *Grandmother's body drops to the ground.*

He's suddenly fighting back tears.

> CESAIRE
> I loved her and Lucie both. I never
> wanted to hurt them.

Valerie's eyes go to her basket on the table.

> CESAIRE
> Come with me. It's the last day of the
> Blood Moon—one bite, and you'll be
> like me...

> VALERIE
> Why don't you just force me?

169

CESAIRE
I need you as an ally, not a slave.

VALERIE
I won't do what you do. I can't.

CESAIRE
Yes, you can, Valerie. My blood
already courses through your veins.
It's a gift. A GIFT my father gave
me that I can now give to you. I'm
stronger than he was, and you'll be
even stronger than me... The world
will lay at our feet. We will be
invincible.

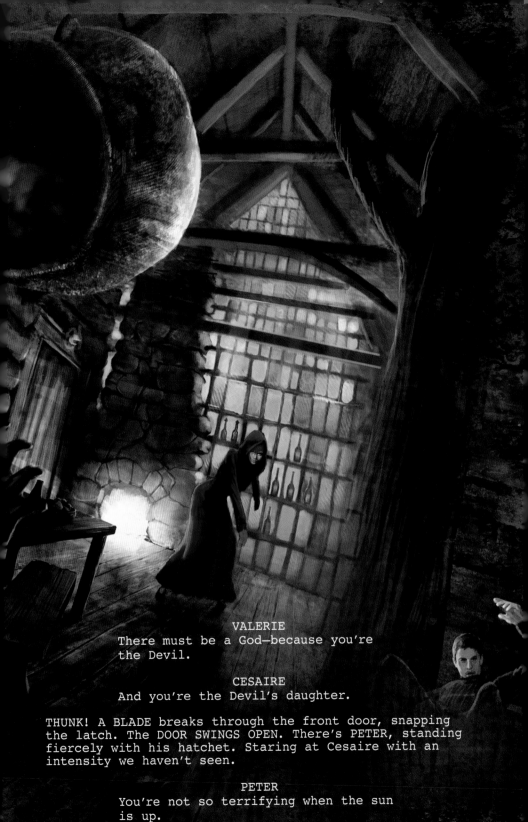

VALERIE
There must be a God—because you're
the Devil.

CESAIRE
And you're the Devil's daughter.

THUNK! A BLADE breaks through the front door, snapping
the latch. The DOOR SWINGS OPEN. There's PETER, standing
fiercely with his hatchet. Staring at Cesaire with an
intensity we haven't seen.

PETER
You're not so terrifying when the sun
is up.

171

Peter charges toward Cesaire with his HATCHET. Cesaire's eyes FLASH with a power that is BEYOND HUMAN. With laser-sharp reflexes, *Cesaire's hand shoots up and stops the hatchet an inch from his forehead.*

> CESAIRE
> How would you know?

Peter and Cesaire grapple with the hatchet, angry and vicious, wrestling, moving so quickly that we can't see what's happening. Cesaire PUNCHES Peter hard—in the face. Peter SWINGS back and connects with Cesaire's jaw. Peter grabs the weapon with two hands to push it into Cesaire's head, but at the last moment Cesaire pushes back, WHIPPING Peter around and FLINGING him across the room, SMASHING into the shelves next to the LOOM.

Glass jars SHATTER across the floor as Peter slumps to the ground. Cesaire LAUNCHES himself onto the deck, going in for the kill, when... he is stopped by a haunting, almost wolflike voice, luring him to turn around.

> VALERIE
> Father...

Cesaire turns, and there is Valerie. Like a dream. In her Red Riding Hood. Holding the basket. This image of his beautiful daughter is perfect. He feels a father's pride.

Cesaire stares, almost transfixed. Behind Cesaire, we see Peter watching Valerie—closely.

> VALERIE (CONT'D)
> I have something for you...

> CESAIRE
> What is it?

> VALERIE
> (gently)
> I'll show you.

Valerie steps forward. Cesaire looks at Peter. He now seems to be unconscious. No threat. Cesaire turns back to Valerie. And with a mixture of curiosity and caution—

> CESAIRE
> Let me see it.

She opens the basket and tilts it toward him, slightly. As Cesaire looks down at it, Valerie glances quickly at Peter, indicating the axe that lays a few feet away.

172

Valerie looks back at Cesaire, who is leaning forward, trying to look into the basket, when THUMP!

THE HATCHET IS NOW IN HIS BACK. PETER HAS THROWN IT.

CESAIRE REACHES BEHIND HIMSELF with both hands to pull out the hatchet. He ROARS in pain. Not human, not animal.

His eyes BURN—THE BEAST IS TRYING TO BREAK THROUGH. The rage is only making him STRONGER, BUT...

                    VALERIE
          I brought you this...

From her basket, she takes SOLOMON'S SEVERED HAND.

FLASH: Valerie at the church. Now, we see that instead of smoothing the snow, she was digging out Solomon's hand.

Cesaire's eyes flick with panic when he sees the RAZOR-SHARP SILVER FINGERNAILS. He makes brief eye contact with her. She is about to break down, but she steels herself, then DRIVES the SILVER NAILS DEEP into his gut.

This is a moment that no daughter should have to face. She is wracked with pain but forces herself to keep the pressure on until the SILVER courses through Cesaire's veins. As his muscles lock up, father and daughter lock eyes one last time... before his pupils dilate.

Then Cesaire falls to the floor, dead.

VALERIE STARES AT HIS INERT BODY. Angry. Horrified. Full of remorse. Tears well in her eyes. She looks unsteady...

Peter steps up and wraps his arms around her. She is still full of anger—but he holds her close until it begins to pass through her. Now she holds him, too.

They look at each other. Deeply connected.

                    VALERIE (CONT'D)
          ...get me out of here... please...
          Just get me out of here.

He takes her hand, leading her away, but HE WINCES IN PAIN. Peter pulls back his torn sleeve.

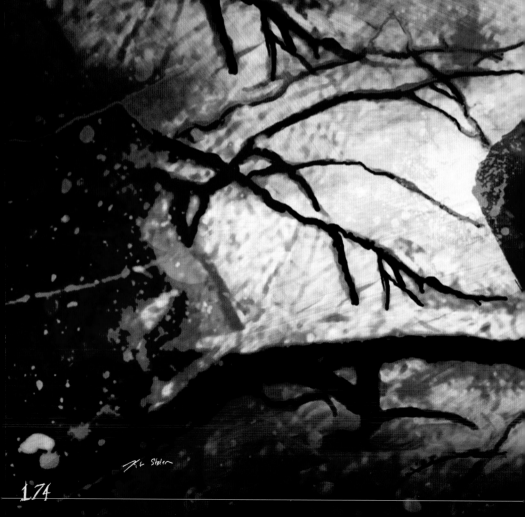

                         PETER
           He bit me.

*FLASH: Cesaire pile-drives his head into Peter's torso. IN
SLOW MOTION: Cesaire twists, then bites Peter's arm.*

Valerie takes Peter's arm and sees the bloody BITE.
Discolored, infected. They look at each other, fully knowing
what this means.

                         VALERIE
           ...Peter...

He shakes his head in disbelief and backs away...

                         PETER
           ...When the Blood Moon rises... I'll be
           like him... a beast...

His head spinning in fear and panic, Peter pushes past
Valerie and charges out the door.

EXT. GRANDMOTHER'S COTTAGE - DAY (SNOW COVERED)

The blizzard over. Tree branches shimmer with frost. Sun reflects off the snow—thousands of blinding diamonds.

Peter crashes down the steps and stumbles into the snow... going to his knees.

And then Valerie is there. On her knees, facing him, looking deep into his eyes. This man links heaven and earth for her.

And now she finds his lips with her mouth. Tears run down her cheeks as her lips softly brush his. Peter returns her kiss. Desperate for her mouth and...

They can't contain themselves any longer. Their hands frantically grope under each other's clothes. Gorgeous predators with burning fingers, hot lips, bare skin...

He pushes her back into the snow and presses against her... temperatures rising, finally indulging their bodies. The RED CLOAK spread beneath them like a DAZZLING CRIMSON ROSE on the LUMINESCENT WHITE-HOT SNOW...

175

EXT.   RIVER BANK - DOCK - LATE AFTERNOON

A stunning half-frozen river. Two figures on a pier. A
small wooden boat moored to a post.

Cesaire's body lies on the dock, next to a pile of
stones. Peter takes out his knife and opens Cesaire's
shirt. Valerie nods. Peter reluctantly lowers the knife
and goes about his unseen task.

Valerie hands him a stone. And another stone. Then
another. And another. Then she crouches down beside
Peter. She feeds black thread into a needle...

EXT.   RIVER - DUSK

Low mist hugs the water. Iridescent in the setting sun.
Slowly, the small wooden boat emerges from the fog.

Peter rows with a long paddle. Valerie sits beside her
father's body—his midsection bulging with the stones. Ice
floes hit the side of the boat.

Halfway across the river, Peter stops rowing.

SPLASH. Cesaire's misshapen body plunges into the water
and sinks quickly out of view... leaving only the deep
indigo void of the river.

EXT.   RIVER BANK - DOCK - DUSK

Peter rows the boat up to the pier. Valerie steps up onto
the deck. She turns to Peter...

...but he's rowing away. Without her.

> VALERIE
> Peter...

Valerie's voice stops Peter, but he doesn't turn around. The sun is setting. He looks at his wounded arm.

Finally, he turns to Valerie. Looks at the one soul he loves in the whole world. It pains him to say it:

> PETER
> I have to leave you... You won't be safe with me... until I learn to control myself.

Valerie's heart seems to rupture.

FLASH: *She sees the abyss, the sun, the stars... she sees herself and Peter climbing mountains, hunting tigers... limbs intertwined with the rise and fall of the tides...*

...but she understands that she has to let him go.

> VALERIE
> ...I'll wait for you...

> PETER
> I thought you'd say that.

Valerie has to smile... But, unable to look at her a moment longer, Peter turns and starts to paddle away.

Valerie watches him go, watches until he vanishes into the fog... glowing in the last golden rays of the sun.

I'll wait for you...

I thought you'd say that.

BEHIND THE SCENES

I want to

the Book

Graphic Designers
Linda Posivak
Dustin Stanton

Layouts
Patrick Sanchez Smith
Nikki Ramey

All Storyboards
Trevor Goring

Kimberly French
Set Photographs
Pages: 1, 16, 17, 20–21, 24–25, 28–29, 30–31,
34–35, 36–37, 46, 52–53, 54, 55, 56–57, 60–61,
62, 64 (left), 66–67, 74–75, 77, 78, 79, 80–81,
82–83, 90–91, 92–93, 102–103, 104–105,
108–109, 110–111, 122–123, 127, 132–133,
135 (bottom right), 136–137, 138–139 (top),
142–143, 146–147, 149, 150–151, 154–155,
156–157, 158–159, 160–161, 166–167, 177, 178,
179, 180–181, 182–183, 184 (all but middle left),
185, 186–187, 188–189, 191–192

Nels Israelson
Cover photography

Dean Sherriff
Set Illustrations
Pages: 2–3, 8–9, 10–11, 12–13 (top),
14–15, 22–23 (top), 26–27, 38–39,
44–45, 46–47, 50–51, 70–71, 94–95,
115, 126, 130–131

Kit Stölen
Costume Illustrations
Pages: 14, 15, 18, 19, 29, 30, 32, 33,
42–43, 63, 79 (top), 100–101 (top),
106–107, 113, 120, 138–139 (bottom);
140–141, 154 (top), 174–175, 183
(top right and right), 191

Linda Posivak

Dustin Stanton

Patrick Smith

Tom Sanders

Sean Harding

Catherine I-ch-

Mandy Walker

Don Macaulay

Kimberly French

Dean Sherriff

182

183

the FILM

WARNER BROS. PICTURES presents

An APPIAN WAY Production

Directed by
CATHERINE HARDWICKE

Sreenplay written by
DAVID LESLIE JOHNSON

Produced by
JENNIFER DAVISSON KILLORAN
LEONARDO DiCAPRIO
JULIE YORN

Executive Producers
JIM ROWE
MICHAEL IRELAND
CATHERINE HARDWICKE

Director of Photography
MANDY WALKER, A.C.S.

Production Designer
TOM SANDERS

Edited by
NANCY RICHARDSON, A.C.E.
JULIA WONG

Music by
BRIAN REITZELL

Visual Effects Supervisor
JEFFREY A. OKUN

Costumes Designed by
CINDY EVANS

Casting by
RONNA KRESS

CAST
Valerie AMANDA SEYFRIED
Father Solomon GARY OLDMAN
Cesaire BILLY BURKE
Peter SHILOH FERNANDEZ
Henry MAX IRONS
Suzette VIRGINIA MADSEN
Grandmother JULIE CHRISTIE
Father Auguste LUKAS HAAS
Roxanne SHAUNA KAIN
Captain ADRIAN HOLMES
Madame Lazar CHRISTINE WILLES
The Reeve MICHAEL HOGAN
Claude COLE HEPPELL
Adrien Lazar MICHAEL SHANKS
Prudence KACEY ROHL
Rose CARMEN LAVIGNE
Tavern Owner DON THOMPSON
Marguerite JENNIFER HALLEY
Young Valerie MEGAN CHARPENTIER
Young Peter DJ GREENBURG
Solomon's Daughters BELLA KING
OLIVIA STEELE-FALCONER
Lucie ALEXANDRIA MAILLOT
Solomon's Soldiers
JAMES MICHALOPOULOS
BRAD KELLY
MATT WARD
PAUL WU
GAVIN BUHR
DARREN SHAHLAVI
DALIAS BLAKE
LAURO CHARTRAND
SAMUEL SMITH
MICHAEL ADAMTHWAITE

2nd Unit Director
ANDY CHENG

Assistant Directors
PAUL BARRY
MISHA BUKOWSKI
TRACEY POIRIER

185

Lighting
DAVE TICKELL
JAMES McMURACHY
PAUL MATSALLA
SAUBRIE MOHAMED
DAN FRASER
JAMES LISTON
JAY DIAMOND
TOM WATSON
SEAN OXENBURY
KURT ZELMER
ROGER WELLS

Grips
MIKE KIRILENKO
DREW DAVID
RYAN MONRO
JAMES KOHNE
LEE GIBEAU
KEVIN LHETERIER
GLEN HAWKINS
DAVID McINTOSH
BIPPEN KUMAR SAMMY

Special FX
JOEL WHIST
DAN CERVIN
SCOTT TREVLIVING
W.A. ANDREW SCULTHORP
STEVE HEPWORTH
JOHN WILKINSON
CORIE TORNACKE
PAUL BENJAMIN

Production Manager
BRENDAN FERSUSON

Production Office
NICOLE OGUCHI
JILL CHRISTENSEN
JILL DYCK

Props
DAN SISSONS
RENATA ZALESKA
DAVE ROSYCHUK

Makeup FX
BILL TEREZAKIS
MAUREEN TEREZAKIS

Stunt Coordinators
ANDY CHENG
SCOTT NICHOLSON

Horse Wrangler
DANNY VIRTUE

Construction
CHARLES LEITRANTS
AL ROURKE
JASON CLARIDGE
BRENT GLOECKLER
DAVID MURRAY
MARK TOMPKINS
SHARON DEVER
ZBIGNIEW SCHELLER

Accounting
JAN DENNEHY
JOANNE WOODWARD
ALEX SKREPNIK
ANNIE DOYAN

Sound Recording
MICHAEL McGEE
DON BROWN
JUNIPER WATTERS

Video Assist
LANCE WHITE

Script Supervisor
KIMI WEBBER

Choreographer
SARAH ELGART

186

2nd Unit (cont'd)
TREVOR CARABIN
GLEN HAWKINS
ELSPETH GRAFTON

thanks to:

WARNER BROS. PICTURES
JEFF ROBINOV
GREG SILVERMAN
LYNN HARRIS
NIIJA KUYKENDALL
STEVE PAPAZIAN
CHRIS DEFARIA
BILL DRAPER
ANNE KOLBE
LORA KENNEDY
PAUL BROUCEK
MARC SOLOMON
SUE KROLL
BLAIR RICH
MASSEY RAFANI
DIANE SPONSLER
STEPHANIE WHEELER
SUSANNAH SCOTT
ELAINE PIECHOWSKI
STEVE FOGELSON

JENNIFER DAVISSON KILLORAN
LEONARDO DiCAPRIO
MICHAEL IRELAND
ALEX MACE
ROWENA ARGUELLES
SPENCER BAUMGARTEN
WARREN DERN
RAND RAVICH
PATRICK SANCHEZ SMITH
NIKKI RAMEY
SARAH BLAKELY-CARTWRIGHT
JAMEE HARDWICKE
JAMIE MARSHALL
MARK JACKSON
NIA MALIKA DIXON
BEN HARDWICKE
JANET GRILLO
RICHARD KIDD
ANDREA BROWN
ALEXANDER MCQUEEN
WEEN

IN MEMORY OF
BARBARA GASIOR

188

189

ABOUT THE SCREENWRITER

David Leslie Johnson was born about as far from Hollywood as one can be. Raised in Mansfield, Ohio, by schoolteacher parents, he developed an early interest in storytelling and began writing plays in the second grade. He later became interested in film and, at age nineteen, wrote his first screenplay. He attended The Ohio State University in Columbus, Ohio, and graduated with a Bachelor of Fine Arts degree in Photography and Cinema.

Not long after, he found himself back in his hometown working as a production assistant on *The Shawshank Redemption*, which was filmed on location at the historic Mansfield Reformatory, where Johnson's great-grandfather had been a prison guard. Determined to make an impression on the visiting film crew, he worked during the day in the editing room and at night began writing a sample screenplay, which he finished on the last day of shooting. The script garnered the attention of Frank Darabont, the film's Academy Award®–nominated director and writer. Johnson spent the next five years as Darabont's assistant, using the opportunity to learn the trade of screenwriting from one of the industry's most respected talents.

Johnson currently has several projects in development. David Johnson lives in Burbank, California, with his wife, screenwriter Kimberly Lofstrom Johnson, and son, Samuel.

ABOUT THE DIRECTOR

Catherine Hardwicke trained as an architect at the University of Texas and started in film as a production designer. She designed over twenty films, including *Tombstone*, *Tank Girl*, *Three Kings*, and *Vanilla Sky*. Hardwicke's debut as a feature film cowriter and director was *Thirteen*. Made for under $2 million, it garnered dozens of accolades, including Best Director at Sundance, an Academy Award® and a Golden Globe® nomination for Holly Hunter, a Golden Globe® nomination for Evan Rachel Wood, and the Independent Spirit Award for Best Breakout Performance for Nikki Reed.

Hardwicke has since directed *Lords of Dogtown*, *The Nativity Story*, and the international hit *Twilight*, based on the best-selling novel by Stephenie Meyer. *Twilight* won six MTV Movie Awards and landed Hardwicke in the Guinness Book of Records for the highest-grossing opening weekend for a female director in film history.

Hardwicke is also the author of the *New York Times* Best Seller *Twilight Director's Notebook*. Hardwicke's most recent film is *Red Riding Hood*, and she is currently developing new projects in Venice, California.

by
Catherine
Hardwicke